Cancún
& Cozumel
DIRECTIONS

WRITTEN AND RESEARCHED BY

Zora O'Neill

ROUGH
GUIDES

NEW YORK • LONDON • DELHI

www.roughguides.com

Contents

Introduction	4

Ideas	9

The big six.. 10
Beaches 12
Diving and snorkelling 14
Bars and lounges.............................. 16
Clubs... 18
Shopping 20
Casual dining..................................... 22
Fine dining.. 24
Romantic Cancún and Cozumel 26
B&Bs and bungalows......................... 28
Hotels 30
Ruins... 32
Natural Cancún and Cozumel 34
Tours and trips 36
Water sports 38
Local culture...................................... 40
Hidden Cancún and Cozumel............ 42
Family fun 44
Festivals and pastimes 46

Places	49

Cancún's zona hotelera.................... 51
Downtown Cancún 67

Isla Mujeres....................................... 78
Puerto Morelos 90
Playa del Carmen 99
Isla Cozumel.................................... 113
Tulum 131
The inland ruins.............................. 144

Essentials	157

Arrrival 159
Information....................................... 159
Transport and tours 160
Costs and money............................ 162
Accommodation............................... 163
Food and drink 164
Sports and outdoor activities 165
Festivals and events 168
Shopping 169
Directory.. 170

Language	173

Index	189

Introduction to

Cancún
& Cozumel

◄ Red macaw

Cancún and Cozumel, the two largest tourist destinations on Mexico's northern Caribbean coast, are for many travellers inexorably linked with glitzy overdevelopment and all-inclusive fun. But from the plane window as you descend into Cancún International Airport, even the grandest megaresort is nearly lost in the azure sea to the east or the jungle stretching west to the horizon like a solid green carpet. This area is still very much the frontier.

Between the developed shoreline, which capitalizes on impeccably white sand and clear water in improbable shades of turquoise, and the wild inland, you'll find remarkable opportunities for recreation. Here you can dive along the second-largest barrier reef in the world, practise yoga on an empty beach, explore overgrown ruins in a jungle teeming with birds and butterflies, and dance till dawn – all in one day.

◄ The Cancún coast

◄ Tulum's seaside ruins

Cancún's reputation for spring break debauchery is deserved – if you've come for relentless, if irresistible entertainment, you've come to the right place – but it offers so much more. Carved out of the jungle in the 1970s as part of a government tourism initiative, it's a purpose-built city that embraces the new. First-time visitors may see a sharp division between the pleasure-seeking *zona hotelera*, or hotel zone, and the more utilitarian mainland downtown, but both Cancúns harbour authentic Mexican culture if you know where to look.

The island of Cozumel has been welcoming international visitors for slightly longer – in the late 1960s, fanatical scuba divers spread the word about the rich and healthy coral reefs that ring its shores. Countless divers enter the ocean in high season, while on land, thousands of cruise-ship passengers disembark nearly every day. Despite the crowds (which have given it a noticeable American accent), the far side of the island remains a rugged, beautiful escape.

▼ Church, Puerto Morelos

Elsewhere along this stretch of coast a series of resorts and villages round out the quintessential beach experience – or provide holiday alternatives altogether. Isla Mujeres, directly off the coast from Cancún, has a distinctly Caribbean feel, while the small town of Puerto Morelos, just half an

▼ Maroma, Puerto Morelos

hour from the airport, has a slow, amiable pace. Playa del Carmen, where the Cozumel ferry docks, has grown into a stylish beach destination for European tourists. And Tulum maintains a bohemian air on its pristine beaches, even as backpackers are outnumbered by wealthier visitors in search of quiet retreat.

If you want more than beaches, an easy day or overnight trip inland offers variety. The seemingly impenetrable jungle has its oases: natural ones, like the freshwater sinkholes called *cenotes*, which are perfect for a refreshing swim, and urban centres like the gracious colonial city of Valladolid. Vestiges of Maya culture are apparent everywhere – preserved most noticeably in the grand ruins at Chichén Itzá, Ek-Balam and Cobá, whose enduring pyramids overshadow any hotel tower.

When to visit

High season, when the weather is sunny and mild, comes in mid-December through April, with prices spiking between Christmas and New Year and in the week before Easter, which is a major holiday week for Mexicans that overlaps with college students on spring break. The **rainy season** starts in late May, with rising temperatures and muggier air. Rain is usually limited to an hour-long afternoon cloudburst, which does more damage to dirt roads than to travel plans. Mid-July through August is another popular vacation time with Mexicans and Europeans – hotel prices in Playa del Carmen and Tulum reflect this demand. From mid-September through mid-November, **hurricanes** are a threat. Many hotels close for October, but those that remain open will offer incredible deals. Expect wet weather and choppy seas (as well as plenty of mosquitoes), if not an actual storm.

Cancún & Cozumel

AT A GLANCE

PLAYA DEL CARMEN

This fast-growing, cosmopolitan town caters to international visitors and hip weekenders jetting in from Mexico City.

COZUMEL

Above the waterline, a busy cruise ship port and destination for bird-watchers; below, an awe-inspiring riot of colour among the coral reefs.

CANCÚN

A glittering, slightly tacky clutch of resorts, clubs, malls and gorgeous beaches alongside a bustling, prosperous city – two faces of modern Mexico.

▲ Diving off the coast of Cozumel

TULUM

Great beaches and distinctive ruins, evolving into a popular resort area for yoga practitioners and others who enjoy cabañas lit by candlelight.

▲ Cancún nightlife

▼ The beach at Tulum

▼ Maya house, Puerto Morelos

▶ Chichén Itzá

PUERTO MORELOS

A quiet throwback to old-style coastal Mexico, still holding strong to its fishing economy and unhurried lifestyle.

CHICHÉN ITZÁ

A trek inland, but a don't-miss archeological site: the emblem of Mayan power on the Yucatán Peninsula.

Ideas

The big six

The attractions of Mexico's Caribbean coast may at first seem strangely juxtaposed: ancient Maya sites stand a short distance from the trendy bars and boutiques of Playa del Carmen's central avenue, while the natural beauty of Cozumel's pristine reefs is evident even amid the glitz of Cancún's *zona hotelera*. This proximity of seemingly disparate elements – of nature and civilization, of the ancient and the modern – is a common theme in and around Cancún, and largely a successful one. The following six experiences are not to be missed.

▼ El Castillo

The giant pyramid that towers over the ruined city of Chichén Itzá is an icon of Maya power in the Yucatán Peninsula – and a very popular tourist site.

P.147 ▶ THE INLAND RUINS

▼ Cancún beaches

All pure white sand and clear turquoise water stretching as far as you can see, Cancun's coastline alone spurred tourist development across the entire region.

P.54 ▶ CANCÚN'S ZONA HOTELERA

▲ Cozumel's reefs

The coral atolls surrounding the island draw diving fanatics who relish some of the richest and most diverse marine life in the world.

P.118 ▸ ISLA COZUMEL

▲ Cenotes

Filled with crystal-clear water, the many caves and sinkholes that dot the peninsula make for an otherworldly swimming experience.

P.91 ▸ PUERTO MORELOS

▼ La Quinta

See and be see on Playa del Carmen's main drag, a casual, cosmopolitan strip lined with shops, hotels and bars.

P.99 ▸ PLAYA DEL CARMEN

▼ Tulum

This Maya city, one of only a few inhabited when the Spanish arrived, is marked by quirky architecture and a beautiful cliff-top setting.

P.131 ▸ TULUM

Beaches

Along Mexico's Caribbean coast you'll find a beach to suit every taste, from deserted stretches with uninterrupted vistas to expansive sandy playgrounds affording full-on fun in the sun. Beach clubs are common, providing umbrellas and chairs, gear rental and activities, often for the price of only a drink or two, while at free public beaches, the only refreshments may come from the occasional strolling vendor. All beaches share one universal feature – powdery white sand that never gets hot underfoot, lapped by turquoise-green waves.

▲ Mamita's Beach Club

Dedicated tanners who love cool DJ beats spend their days at this deep beachfront.

P.101 ▸ PLAYA DEL CARMEN

▲ Chen Río

A rare tame spot on the island's rugged, windswept eastern shore, the Chen Río beach club is often deserted – save for a bartender mixing margaritas.

P.122 ▸ ISLA COZUMEL

▲ Playa Norte

The long, shallow stretch across the north end of Isla Mujeres is great for wading, lounging and savouring drinks at sunset.

P.80 ▶ ISLA MUJERES

▶ Nachi-Cocom

Check out this classy club with a gorgeous beach, a vast swimming pool and an elegant restaurant.

P.120 ▶ ISLA COZUMEL

▲ El Paraíso Beach Club

Tulum's backpacker crowd comes here for funky music and inexpensive drinks – and the mellow party often carries on after sundown.

P.134 ▶ TULUM

▼ Playa Delfines

Cancún's showpiece public beach has the occasional big wave, as it's on the open Caribbean, which stretches to the horizon in dazzling hues.

P.55 ▶ CANCÚN'S ZONA HOTELERA

Diving and snorkelling

As alluring as the beaches here are, the scenery only gets better below the waterline. Offshore lies the rich marine life of the Mesoamerican Barrier Reef, much of which is protected in national parks. The coral growth is stunning, particularly around Cozumel, but an array of experiences, for scuba divers of all levels, can be found all along the coast.

▼ Caves

Only more advanced divers should enter enclosed spaces – but the sights, such as the legendary "sleeping" sharks off the coast of Isla Mujeres, more than reward their efforts.

P.83 ▸ ISLA MUJERES

▼ Wreck dives

Ghost ships lurking on the sea floor provide a home for shy sea critters – and a fascinating realm for divers to explore.

P.90 ▸ PUERTO MORELOS

▼ Marine life

Catch an up-close glimpse of the region's spectacular and thriving marine life, from giant leatherback sea turtles to majestic eagle rays.

P.119 ▶ ISLA COZUMEL

▲ Coral gardens

Novice divers and snorkellers alike can enjoy these shallow, protected beds of coral that are breeding grounds for dazzling fish.

P.118 ▶ COZUMEL

Bars and lounges

Whether you want to groove to a jazz trio or just sip a margarita and relax in the balmy night, there's a bar to suit your taste somewhere in or around Cancún. In smaller towns, hotel beach bars offer generous happy hours to smooth the transition from sunbathing to dancing in the sand. Not all the action's at the beach, however. Lounges oozing cool in Cancún, Playa del Carmen and Cozumel will, with their live music and lavish drinks, do what might seem impossible – make you want to change out of your swimsuit for a visit.

▲ Ula-Gula

From your perch in this cosy candlelit bar in Playa, you can enjoy strong tropical cocktails and a view of the parade of partygoers in the street.

P.111 ▸ PLAYA DEL CARMEN

▲ El Camarote

Old-style Mexican crooners take the stage at this intimate, atmospheric Cancún bar, a favourite with an older, bohemian crowd.

P.76 ▸ DOWNTOWN CANCÚN

▲ Papaya Playa

A perpetual soundtrack of groovy electronica draws young globe-trotters to this laid-back beach hotel and its big bar under a rustic palm-thatch roof.

P.139 ▶ TULUM

▼ Trágara

Sink into a sofa to watch the sun go down at this hip lounge on the lagoon in Cancún. The cocktails come in fiery colours to match the show in the sky.

P.64 ▶ CANCÚN'S ZONA HOTELERA

▲ Roots

Cancún's best live music venue books excellent jazz acts – including some internationally known names – but retains an informal, funky ambiance.

P.77 ▶ DOWNTOWN CANCÚN

Clubs

Clubbing reaches its zenith in Cancún, where no expense is spared to create an eye-popping and ear-thumping spectacle. In Playa del Carmen, the mood is mellower and the attitude more casual, but you'll still find places on the beach dedicated to seeing the night through to sunrise, accompanied by more diverse music. And the fun is by no means just for tourists – locals go out to dance, too, particularly at a few excellent salsa clubs.

▼ The City

The party goes literally round-the-clock at this Cancún hot spot: chill at the beach club by day; dance till dawn to a pulsing sound system; repeat.

P.65 ▸ CANCÚN'S ZONA HOTELERA

▲ Coco Bongo

Over-the-top entertainment is the unabashed goal at Cancún's most popular nightspot, a multilevel place with elaborate sound and dazzling lights and performances.

P.65 ▸ CANCÚN'S ZONA HOTELERA

▲ La Santanera

Playa's most stylish gather at this bi-level club and lounge that's known for its excellent music and even surprise shows by top international DJs.

P.112 ▸ PLAYA DEL CARMEN

▼ Glazz

The more intimate nightlife option in Cancún – not just a black-lit dance floor, but also a cool cocktail bar with comfy nooks to lounge in.

P.65 ▸ CANCÚN'S ZONA HOTELERA

▼ Mambo Café

The excellent Cuban bands at Cancún's largest salsa club inspire local dancers to cut loose on the expansive wooden dance floor.

P.77 ▸ DOWNTOWN CANCÚN

Shopping

If you're a shopper, bring an extra bag to carry your purchases home: Cancún is packed with malls stocked with luxury goods, Cozumel is aswim in duty-free deals, and all along the coast whimsical craft shops are jam-packed with wooden masks, striped blankets, beautiful embroidery and silver jewellery accented with opals, turquoise or amber. But don't overlook the kitsch: surely someone at home will appreciate a purple-and-gold velvet sombrero.

▲ La Calaca

A whimsical, colourful arts and craft selection from all over Mexico is presented with care at this excellent, reasonably priced shop.

P.106 ▸ PLAYA DEL CARMEN

▲ Los Cinco Soles

Of all the seafront souvenir emporiums in San Miguel, Los Cinco Soles has the best-quality stock, particularly its beautiful jewellery and housewares.

P.125 ▸ ISLA COZUMEL

▲ Mercado 23

Get a taste of old Mexico at this collection of densely packed market stalls stocking everything from fresh vegetables to cattle feed.

P.73 ▸ DOWNTOWN CANCÚN

▲ Paseo del Carmen

This chic open-air mall deals in trendy Euro brands and high-end Mexican design – it's the first place to go for a cool new bikini.

P.107 ▸ PLAYA DEL CARMEN

▼ El Aguacate

The name *El Aguacate* is famous peninsula-wide for its skillfully woven hammocks. Can't decide on a colour? Try cutting a deal for a few.

P.74 ▸ DOWNTOWN CANCÚN

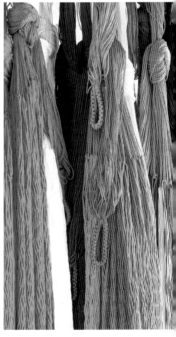

▼ Alma Libre

For beach reads or a Maya language reader, browse this inviting bookshop which has exceptionally helpful owners.

P.96 ▸ PUERTO MORELOS

Casual dining

Getting an authentic taste of Mexico's Caribbean coast is as easy as walking to the nearest beachfront shack serving fresh ceviche made from fish just plucked from the sea. In town, head to the nearest plaza, where vendors dole out tasty and cheap *antojitos* – the name for any corn-based snack, from cheesy quesadillas to tamales steamed in banana leaves to meaty tacos. Those dedicated to inexpensive, authentic eats will find set-price lunch deals are gut-busting bargains.

▲ La Floresta

The best shrimp tacos in Playa may be nowhere near the beach, but this road-side restaurant is well worth the trip for a savoury lunch.

P.108 ▸ PLAYA DEL CARMEN

▲ Cockteleria Picus

Make your first stop off the ferry this little wooden shack on the sand that specializes in fresh ceviche and shrimp cocktails.

P.87 ▸ ISLA MUJERES

◀ Sabores

Sample excellent home cooking, literally – the chef-owner serves up generous portions in the back garden of her own house.

P.129 ▸ ISLA COZUMEL

▶ Parque de las Palapas

Cancún's main park, where stalls sell a delicious array of snacks, is a sociable and economical place to dine after dark.

P.67 ▸ DOWNTOWN CANCÚN

▼ Playa Lancheros

Grilled fish can't get any simpler or tastier than at this beachside open-air grill staffed by dedicated cooks who practically grew up here.

P.82 ▸ ISLA MUJERES

Fine dining

Eating out in the Yucatán isn't all about tacos and enchiladas – some of the best food on the coast is produced by chefs taking licence with centuries-old dishes. At the same time, some long-established expats from Italy and the United States have put their spin on things, running restaurants that serve serious food but retain the fun, relaxed vibe of the beach towns that lured them in the first place.

▲ Yaxche

Traditional Maya cuisine gets a respectful makeover at this classy restaurant – close the meal with a show-stopping "café Maya".

P.111 ▸ PLAYA DEL CARMEN

▲ La Habichuela

Quiet and elegant, particularly in the golden-lit garden, this romantic restaurant uses Caribbean flavours such as tamarind and coconut to impressive effect.

P.76 ▸ DOWNTOWN CANCÚN

▲ Pancho's Backyard

Gracious service is the hallmark of this big, refined Mexican restaurant set in a beautiful old house in San Miguel.

P.128 ▸ ISLA COZUMEL

▼ La Casa de las Margaritas

A typically showy Cancún restaurant – but the bartenders' stunts shouldn't distract from the exquisite regional Mexican specialities.

P.62 ▸ CANCÚN'S ZONA HOTELERA

▲ John Gray's Kitchen

A gem of a find in quiet Puerto Morelos, the restaurant's eponymous chef cooks inventive but satisfying international food.

P.98 ▸ PUERTO MORELOS

◀ Posada Margherita

The beachfront setting and convivial service may seem casual, but the perfectly executed Italian dishes put this restaurant on the must-visit list.

P.142 ▸ TULUM

Romantic Cancún and Cozumel

With balmy ocean breezes, bountiful flowering trees and gorgeous vistas, the warmth of Cancún and Cozumel effortlessly inspires romance. Cosy restaurants and secluded hotels further add to the amorous mood, aided by a strongly sentimental strain in the local culture – dreamy *trova* music.

▼ La Madonna

Hide away at a secluded balcony table at this high-style bar where the lights are low and the drinks are strong.

P.64 ▶ CANCÚN'S ZONA HOTELERA

▲ Azulik

Harbouring a treehouse fantasy? Snuggle by candlelight at one of these de luxe cabins on the cliffs.

P.136 ▸ TULUM

◀ Casa Rolandi

A stunning view of the bay and beach sets the passionate tone at this isolated Italian restaurant.

P.87 ▸ ISLA MUJERES

▼ Alux

Make-out nooks abound at this groovy nightclub in a cave, where a nightly belly dancing show enhances the naturally steamy atmosphere.

P.111 ▸ PLAYA DEL CARMEN

B&Bs and bungalows

Defined by their owners' quirks and tastes, these cosy accommodations make you feel like you're visiting friends – who, in many cases, just happen to have prime beachfront property and cook delicious breakfasts. Whether traditional palm-thatch cabañas or made of sturdier concrete, most of these guesthouses seem like natural extensions of the landscape. Although Cancún has only a couple of these more intimate places to stay, there's a bounty of them along the rest of the coast.

▼ Villa Las Brisas

Friendly owners, a fabulous breakfast and carefully designed rooms – all the hallmarks of a great B&B, plus a fine away-from-it-all location.

P.86 ▶ ISLA MUJERES

▲ Sak Ol

Spacious, comfortable rooms help contribute to the very relaxed vibe at this small resort, where the most popular activity is getting a massage.

P.96 ▸ PUERTO MORELOS

▲ Coco's Cabañas

Although tiny, *Coco's* has everything you need to relax – a pool, an excellent restaurant and a quiet beach just steps away.

P.95 ▸ PUERTO MORELOS

▼ Nueva Vida de Ramiro

Thanks to the owners' determination not to cut trees for expansion, the wood cabins with big front decks here feel very private.

P.138 ▸ TULUM

▼ Tamarindo

Get beautifully designed rooms at bargain rates, plus a big, private walled garden at this San Miguel B&B.

P.124 ▸ ISLA COZUMEL

Hotels

With thousands of hotel beds to choose from, visitors are spoiled for choice in Cancún and along the coast. There's no typical hotel: they range from intimate, family-run establishments to three-hundred-room towers operated by international chains. The best of the latter luxuriate in their Caribbean surroundings but draw on international standards of service.

▲ Le Meridien

Subdued luxury is the hallmark at this French-run hotel – although the multilevel swimming pool is deliciously decadent.

P.58 ▶ CANCÚN'S ZONA HOTELERA

▼ Las Anclas

At this small suite hotel in San Miguel, dedicated owners lovingly attend to every detail – from flowers in the rooms to dinner choices – and ensure that your stay will be a memorable one.

P.122 › ISLA COZUMEL

▲ Kinbé

A prime location, midway between the beach and the main drag, is the big bonus at this cute Italian-run hotel.

P.105 › PLAYA DEL CARMEN

▼ Maroma

Of the class of hotels that welcome you with a margarita, *Maroma* is the best – impeccably designed, and lavish without being ostentatious.

P.95 › PUERTO MORELOS

▲ Deseo

Enjoy the poolside conjuring up Miami Beach and rooms made for lounging at *Deseo*, designed for the partying Playa visitor.

P.105 › PLAYA DEL CARMEN

Ruins

Although El Castillo, the great pyramid at Chichén Itzá, is perhaps the most easily recognized of the Maya remains, it is far from typical of the civilization's style. Spanning almost ten centuries in the Yucatán (see box, p.147), the ancient Maya left behind a range of architectural design that is impressively diverse. So too is the level of restoration at sites – whereas Chichén Itzá is a manicured, well-attended site, the ruins at Cobá and San Gervasio are still partially covered in jungle and home to thriving wildlife.

▲ Ek-Balam

The main attraction at this little-visited ruined city is the flawlessly preserved stucco decoration, which reveals a more personal side of ancient Maya culture.

P.151 ▸ THE INLAND RUINS

▲ Tulum

The enigmatic "diving god" is just one of the idiosyncrasies of this popular site, the richest one along the coast.

P.131 ▸ TULUM

▼ San Gervasio

Cozumel's only restored ruins are worth a visit primarily for the dense surrounding forest, which teems with birds and butterflies.

P.118 ▸ ISLA COZUMEL

▲ El Rey

The only major Maya ruins in Cancún are just a short walk away from the *zona hotelera*'s contemporary glass pyramids.

P.56 ▸ CANCÚN'S ZONA HOTELERA

▶ Chichén Itzá

Toltec influence – in the form of grisly sacrificial platforms, for instance – marks the Yucatán's grandest Maya city.

P.147 ▸ THE INLAND RUINS

▶ Cobá

As the tallest pyramid in the Yucatán, Cobá's Nohoch Mul is not an easy climb, but the vista at the top – dense jungle sprawling to the horizon – is worth every step.

P.152 ▸ THE INLAND RUINS

Natural Cancún and Cozumel

Beyond the tourist hot spots, the Yucatán Peninsula is still a very wild place, and it's easy to travel out into empty stretches of land – empty of humans, that is. The land and sea are heavily populated with all manner of mammals, birds and fish, which you have a better chance of seeing if you wake up early and walk or swim quietly. And while you may enjoy the solitude of the region's more untouched sections alone, you'll learn a lot more if you go with an experienced guide.

▲ Paseo de Manglares

Explore these mangrove-formed swamps teeming with birds and crocodiles from the safety of the boardwalk at the *Ceiba del Mar* hotel.

P.93 ▸ PUERTO MORELOS

▲ Parque Punta Sur

Endangered sea turtles find safe haven at this research station and park, which helps the late-summer hatchlings make it to the sea.

P.121 ▸ ISLA COZUMEL

▼ Isla Contoy

On-site researchers lead bird-watching tours at this small island north of Isla Mujeres that is a sanctuary for pelicans and other sea fowl.

P.84 ▸ ISLA MUJERES

▼ Reserva de la Biósfera Sian Ka'an

Lagoons rich with fish are just one of the several ecosystems contained within this enormous nature reserve, one of Mexico's largest.

P.135 ▸ TULUM

▲ Reserva de Monos Araños

A large population of nimble spider monkeys congregates near Punta Laguna in this reserve dedicated to maintaining the monkeys' habitat.

P.153 ▸ THE INLAND RUINS

Tours and trips

While it's easy enough to travel independently along the coast, organized tours abound – and not all of them are of the mass-market coach variety. An experienced guide can be especially informative for those interested in indigenous fauna and flora or traditional Maya culture, while sportier outings, like boat trips, can be more affordable, as well as more fun, in a small group.

▼ Sailing

Bahía Mujeres, the bay that opens up in front of Cancún, is a gorgeous setting for a sunset outing on a small sailboat.

P.167 ▸ ESSENTIALS

▼ Buggy trips

Home-built dune buggies make for a rough-and-tumble ride into the wilds of Cozumel's north end.

P.162 ▶ ESSENTIALS

▲ Eco-tours

A number of operators specialize in educational trips to explore the peninsula's native forests and to experience local Maya culture.

P.162 ▶ ESSENTIALS

▼ Aerial tours

Get a new perspective on the Caribbean coast from a small plane or ultra-light – tours buzz just over Playa, or as far inland as Chichén Itzá.

P.161 ▶ ESSENTIALS

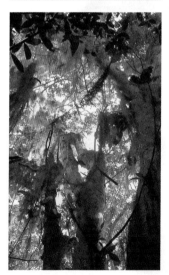

▲ "Jungle" tours

On Cancún's most popular day-trip, travel through the lush lagoon mangroves on a mini-speedboat, then out to sea to snorkel.

P.167 ▶ ESSENTIALS

Water sports

Whether in the wild Caribbean Sea, on a glassy lagoon or in the crystalline waters of an inland cenote, aquaphiles will find plenty to do during their stay. There's a plethora of diving and snorkeling opportunities, and you don't have to look too far either to get your fix – most beachfront hotels offer a range of water activities that are usually available to non-guests as well.

▼ Fishing

Hooking a marlin or a bonefish is a popular pastime in the bay waters and flat lagoons around Cancún, Puerto Morelos or the Sian Ka'an reserve.

P.167 ▸ ESSENTIALS

▲ Cave diving

A risky but rewarding sport, scuba diving in the peninsula's vast underground cave systems reveals fantastical rock formations in perfectly clear water.

P.135 ▶ TULUM

▼ Kayaking

Paddle the centuries-old Maya canals that crisscross the Reserva de la Biósfera Sian Ka'an – just one of the many serene spots along the coast.

P.135 ▶ TULUM

▼ Kiteboarding

Steady breezes and open water have helped forge a strong local community of fans of this developing sport; one popular beach is just south of Cancún.

P.93 ▶ PUERTO MORELOS

▲ Surfing

The strong currents of the open Caribbean can create sizeable waves – especially at Punta Morena on Cozumel.

P.122 ▶ ISLA COZUMEL

Local culture

Although few visitors to Cancún or Cozumel set foot in a museum during their stay, a couple of gems are well worth stepping out of the sun for. And, if you'd prefer to experience Mexican culture away from the exhibits, simply head for a local church, theatre or bullring, where there is no shortage of colourful and compelling pageantry.

▼ Iglesia de San Miguel

Visit Cozumel's main church to see a sixteenth-century wooden statue of Saint Michael that was unearthed on the grounds.

P.115 ▸ ISLA COZUMEL

▼ Museo de la Isla de Cozumel

Covering history, ecology and archeology, Cozumel's tidy museum furnishes an excellent introduction to the island's past.

P.115 ▸ ISLA COZUMEL

▲ Plaza de Toros

The weekly bullfight at Cancún's covered arena – the most frequently used in Mexico – is heralded by an animated musical procession.

P.70 ▶ DOWNTOWN CANCÚN

▼ Ballet Folklórico Nacional de México

Catch this renowned troupe performing an elaborate show of dances from around Mexico – not entirely traditional, but impressive nonetheless.

P.66 ▶ CANCÚN'S ZONA HOTELERA

Hidden Cancún and Cozumel

Even as development on Mexico's Caribbean coast continues apace, a few quiet spots remain – a tiny reservation-only restaurant, a solitary hotel on an empty beach, a refreshing spring veiled by the dense jungle or a campsite that all but blends into the surrounding forest. And some hidden spots, like a funky breakfast café in Playa del Carmen, simply *feel* hidden, even though they're still only steps away from the action.

▼ Boca Paila Camps

A dedication to environmental education distinguishes this excellent tent lodge just inside the Reserva de la Biósfera Sian Ka'an.

P.137 ▸ TULUM

▼ La Cueva del Chango

Hike up the beach from town to this leafy garden, where you can enjoy tasty breakfast and house-roasted coffee.

P.108 ▸ PLAYA DEL CARMEN

▲ Ruta de los Cenotes

Inland from Puerto Morelos, the land is dotted with several beautiful swimming holes, or cenotes, that you'll have all to yourself.

P.91 ▸ PUERTO MORELOS

▼ Ventanas al Mar

Gaze down at the crashing surf from a balcony at this wonderfully remote hotel, the only one on Cozumel's eastern shore.

P.125 ▸ ISLA COZUMEL

Family fun

The Yucatán Peninsula is very much a child-friendly place, with kids not just welcome but doted on nearly everywhere. Throughout the region, family resorts cater to a range of needs, from all-inclusives with busy programmes for kids to laid-back beach haunts where little ones can run wild. Add to this the family entertainment dotted along the coast – particularly the huge nature and water parks of Xcaret and Xel-Há (see p.135) – and you have a vacation destination that will keep youngsters fascinated and entertained.

▼ Parque Chankanaab

Introduce the kids to snorkelling in the quiet lagoon brimming with colourful fish at this well-groomed beach park.

P.119 ▸ ISLA COZUMEL

▲ La Posada del Capitán Lafitte

Let the lids roam free at this easy-going resort, which feels like a rustic summer camp, with a wide beach and a low-tech game room.

P.96 ▶ PUERTO MORELOS

▲ Xcaret

The diversions are endless at this nature park midway down the coast, from horseback riding to cavern snorkelling to visiting a beautiful bay teeming with fish.

P.103 ▶ PLAYA DEL CARMEN

▼ Atlantis

Children can play at Captain Nemo on this submarine that tours the west coast of Cozumel and makes for a novel way to take in the gorgeous reefs.

P.161 ▶ ESSENTIALS

▼ Sunscape Tulum

The children's activity roster is particularly full at this family all-inclusive – leaving parents time for romantic dinners alone.

P.140 ▶ TULUM

Festivals and pastimes

Festivities abound in and around Cancún, whether at a small town's celebration of its patron saint or in the nationwide party that marks the anniversary of Mexico's independence. Cancún also hosts a number of international festivals that showcase the region's renowned music and food.

Although hotels and beaches will be more crowded if you come during a local celebration, it's well worth the additional planning to experience one of the area's many enjoyable annual events.

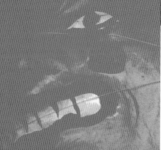

▲ Baseball season

From spring through midsummer, the local baseball field is the place to spend a balmy evening or Sunday afternoon.

P.168 ▶ ESSENTIALS

▲ Día de la Independencia

National pride reaches fever pitch as Mexicans pour into the streets at midnight on September 15 to commemorate the uprising against Spain in 1810.

P.168 ▶ ESSENTIALS

▼ Día de los Muertos

In a tender yet surprisingly buoyant annual ritual, Mexicans honour their dead with graveside picnics and parades of skeletons.

P.169 ▸ ESSENTIALS

▼ Vernal and autumnal equinoxes

Pagans rejoice twice yearly as the sun creates a great serpent-shaped shadow on the staircase of the looming Castillo at Chichén Itzá.

P.168 ▸ ESSENTIALS

▲ Carnaval

The week before Lent, usually in mid-February, is celebrated all along the coast – but the costumes are flashiest and the parades the longest in Cozumel.

P.168 ▸ ESSENTIALS

Places

Cancún's zona hotelera

The **zona hotelera**, or hotel zone, a strip of resorts, clubs, malls and other tourist attractions along a narrow, twenty-five-kilometre-long barrier island that juts out from the mainland, is the part of Cancún most visitors come to experience. Edged by miles of flawless white-sand beaches, it's a high-energy resort destination, relentlessly dedicated to entertaining two million tourists every year with jet skis, top-volume mariachis and wet T-shirt contests. Restaurants are elaborate theatre where waiters at even casual Italian restaurants wear togas, and hotels are fantastical pleasure palaces in a constant state of reinvention. Whether you choose to participate in the myriad activities or simply laze about in the sun, the beaches are undeniably gorgeous, and package-hotel deals (which are increasingly not all-inclusive) can be very reasonable. Moreover, should you choose to leave your manicured compound, you can find authentic Mexican taco stands, salsa clubs and bare-bones beach bars, mainly frequented by friendly locals who are proud of the prosperity that the hotels represent.

La Casa del Arte Popular Mexicano

El Embarcadero centre, Blvd Kuku-Icán Km 4 ☎998/849-4332. Daily 9am–9pm. $5. This lively folk-art museum is crammed with musical instruments, children's toys and colourful traditional costumes. Although the collection, grouped by craft and filling two large rooms, isn't particularly academic or rigorously presented, it does contain some beautiful pieces, such as some elaborate tree-of-life sculptures and beautifully painted gourds.

▼PLAYA DELFINES

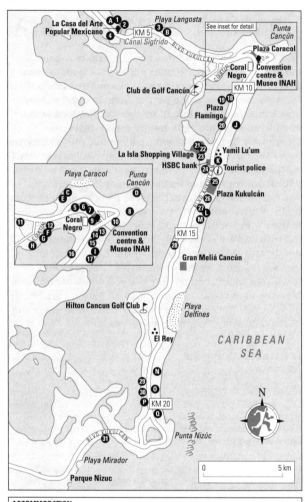

ACCOMMODATION

Ambiance Villas at Kin-Ha	**C**	Dreams Cancun Grand Royal Lagoon	**F**	El Pueblito	**D**	Suites Sina	**H**
Aquamarina		Imperial Laguna		Ritz-Carlton		Villas Manglar	**P**
Beach Hotel	**A**	Le Meridien		Cancún	**G**	Villas Tacul	**L**
Aristos	**O**	El Presidente		Sheraton Cancún	**M**	Westin Resort &	**B**
Avalon Baccará	**J**	Inter-Continental		Resort & Towers		Spa Cancún	**K**
				Suites Girasol	**E**		**I**

EATING AND DRINKING

100% Natural	**25**	La Casa de las		El Galeón		La Madonna	**22**
Azúcar	**8**	Margaritas	**21**	del Caribe	**29**	Over 30 Club	**18**
Ballet Folklórico		Casa Rolandi	**6**	Glazz	**23**	El Rincón Yucateco	**5**
Nacional de		The City	**13**	G-Spot	**19**	Río Nizúc	**31**
México	**9**	Checándole	**20**	Hard Rock Café	**15**	The Royal Bandstand	**26**
Batacha	**17**	Coco Bongo	**14**	Hanaichi	**7**	Señor Frog's	**16**
La Boom	**4**	La Destilería	**24**	JC Capitán	**30**	Trágara	**28**
Bulldog Café	**10**	Dolcemente		Lobby Bar at the		Teatro de Cancún	**1**
Captain Hook	**2**	Pompei	**3**	Ritz-Carlton	**27**	Ty-Coz	**11 & 12**

Visiting the zona hotelera

GreenLine runs a **shared van** service that departs regularly from the airport to destinations throughout the *zona hotelera* ($9 to any hotel); buy tickets from booths positioned directly after customs. **Taxis** are a more direct and expensive option, starting at $17 for the zone closest to the airport.

If there's something you like the look of, chances are you'll be able to pick up a similar item in the excellent gift shop; there's also a bookstore with a good music collection.

Canal Sigfrido

Blvd Kukulcán Km 4.4, immediately east of the bridge by El Embarcadero. A pretty, paved walkway along this channel into the lagoon gives you an up-close view of the dense mangroves that cluster in the brackish water inside the *zona hotelera*'s barrier island. This is a good spot to just sit and watch the water traffic, as fishing tours and pleasure boats cruise by all day, and, if you're especially committed to relaxing, bring your hammock to hang in the thatch-roof palapas provided for shade. Though you might occasionally see kids swimming here, don't be tempted: crocodiles are still quite plentiful in the lagoon.

Playa Langosta

Blvd Kukulcán Km 5. The best of the bay-facing public beaches, Playa Langosta is a sizeable stretch of sand, with calm, clean water for swimming and a few trees for shade – though it can be hard to find a place to lay your towel on weekends. For refreshments, the adjacent tourist pier, packed with bars and shops, is both handy and well stocked with a variety of options.

Playa Tortugas

Blvd Kukulcán Km 7. Very similar to Playa Langosta, but somewhat smaller, this public beach is also neighbour to a giant pier and entertainment complex, anchored by *Fat Tuesday's*, a Mardi Gras-theme party bar. If the crowds get to be too much, head to the eastern edge of the beach, past the pier, where an informal, wood-deck restaurant and bar serves simply grilled seafood and cold beers.

Punta Cancún

At the bend in the *zona hotelera* is the district's heaviest concentration of restaurants, bars and clubs, and the source of the nightlife frenzy that Cancún is famous for. In high season, by about 11pm, Boulevard (or

▼CANAL SIGFRIDO

The beaches

The majority of Cancún's legendary beaches are spread out along the barrier island's northern and eastern shores. The **north side** of the island faces the tranquil Bahía de Mujeres, where the shallow, pale-green water makes an ideal spot for relaxed swimming – particularly for younger children. Sea grass grows in places on this stretch – not the ideal scenery, but it's no impediment to swimming, and is often home to bright tropical fish. Rocks and cliffs break up the sand at Km 6 and Km 8.5 of Boulevard Kukulcán, and continue around the point to Km 9.5. Kayaking is a popular diversion here, and at the west end of this stretch boat traffic is light, so it's a good place for novices to practise windsurfing or kiteboarding (see pp.166–7 for schools, as well as details on other water sports and tours in Cancún).

The island's scenic **east side** – more than 10km of uninterrupted soft, white sand – faces the open Caribbean. While the turquoise ocean waters here appear much more inviting, the waves are sometimes high, and unpredictable currents are a real danger – pay close attention to the daily colour-coded flags, and don't swim beyond your comfort zone. In either case, plan on hitting the beach in the morning, as the east-facing beaches in particular are in shadow from the hotel towers by late afternoon; the *Westin* (see p.60), however, has a small **west-facing** beach.

All of Cancún's beaches are technically open to the public, but **hotels** carefully guard their chairs and umbrellas against interlopers. If you're staying downtown or at a lagoon-side hotel, or simply want a change of scenery from your resort, you have a couple of options. Beachfront bars and clubs, such as *Fat Tuesday's* (Blvd Kukulcán Km 6), *The City* (see p.65) and the *Hard Rock Café* (see p.64), offer lounge chairs and umbrellas that you may use for the price of a drink or an entrance fee (at *The City*). You can also arrange to parasail or rent a jet ski. Bear in mind, however, that a spot in the sand at one of these beaches comes with a loud party atmosphere.

The ten designated **public beach areas**, dotted at intervals along the full length of the *zona hotelera*, have been encroached on by high-rise neighbours, so that many of the turquoise-and-white Fonatur signs now point to not much more than a public walkway and access point between condo developments. A few are worth visiting, however, and these are described in detail in this chapter.

Paseo) Kukulcán is clogged with meandering, scantily dressed fun-seekers and club touts selling open-bar deals, and the party generally lasts – inside the clubs and out – till 4 or 5 in the morning.

East of the nightlife, on the grounds of *Dreams Cancún* (see p.57), is Punta Cancún proper, the easternmost spot in Mexico. Where the point juts into the sea is marked by a whimsical circle of purple blocks – the work of Mexican architect Ricardo Legorreta, who designed the resort. It opened in 1975 as *El Camino Real*, and is still one of Cancún's most distinctive retreats, worth a stroll through to admire the internal hallways filled with greenery and the doors and windows framed with vibrant colours.

Museo INAH

West side of the convention centre ☏998/883-0305. Mon–Sat 9am–8pm, Sun 10am–7pm. $3. This small museum, run by the national archeology institute, presents a limited but absorbing collection of Mesoamerican and Mayan archeological finds, many from sites near Cancún and Tulum. Information, where it's provided at all, is in Spanish, but some of the most fascinating items speak for themselves: delicately wrought clay masks, elaborate zoomorphic incense burners, glowing jade jewellery, and skulls sporting filed-down teeth and drilled with tiny holes. There's usually an English-speaking assistant on hand to answer questions.

Yamil Lu'um

Blvd Kukulcán Km 12. Free. Sandwiched between the *Sheraton* and the *Park Royal Pirámides* (walk through the lobby of either hotel and out to the grounds between) are the remains of two modest Late Post-Classic Maya structures. Both buildings echo styles present at Tulum: the walls of the Templo del Alacrán, named for a scorpion sculpture found inside (now removed), flare outward; while the miniature Adoratoria de la Huello is a small-scale shrine similar to those further down the coast. That said, the land which they occupy and the view it presents is the best reason to visit them

– Yamil Lu'um ("hilly land") refers to the ruins' location on the highest point in Cancún.

Gran Meliá Cancún

Blvd Kukulcán Km 16.5. The vast atrium lobby of this mega-resort cum neo-Mayan pyramid wins the city's unofficial prize for over-the-top opulence. From the giant friezes of ancient deities outside to the interior bursting with cascading plants, koi ponds and waterfalls – as well as dazzled tourists – it's the pinnacle of Cancún's particular brand of excess.

Playa Delfines

Blvd Kukulcán Km 17.5. The first public beach that you see on the way from the airport is also the largest. Occupying a sizeable break between hotel developments, Playa Delfines is a wide, sloping stretch of powder-fine sand fronted by incredible turquoise waters and offering an impressive view up the coast. Like the other beaches which face the open sea, the waves can be particularly high here, so sunbathing is the main activity, though it's sometimes possible to surf. Occasional strolling

▼LOBBY, GRAN MELIÁ CANCÚN

▲PARQUE NIZUC

fruit vendors provide the only services.

El Rey

Blvd Kukulcán Km 18. Daily 8am–5pm. $3. Though El Rey comprises Cancún's largest Maya remains, you may find yourself alone, save for the enormous iguana population, when you visit them. The Late Post-Classic buildings – contemporary with Tulum and San Gervasio on Cozumel – are strung out on a north–south axis alongside Nichupté Lagoon. Objects found during excavation suggest this was a stop on the highly developed sea-trade route around the peninsula, disrupted when the Spanish arrived in the early sixteenth century. Not much of this once-thriving city remains – the ruined structures are mostly small-scale residential buildings, with no impressive pyramids to speak of. With the glass-topped pyramid of the *Hilton* looming in the background, El Rey now functions as a quiet, scenic spot for contemplating the rise and fall of civilizations.

Punta Nizúc

Near Blvd Kukulcán Km 20. At the southern tip of the *zona hotelera*, the reef offshore from Punta Nizúc is the main spot for snorkelling and diving in Cancún. While it's primarily (and most easily) reached by boat with a tour group, you can also reach it by land. The point is on the grounds of *Club Med*, which isn't open to non-guests; instead, walk through the *Westin*, then turn right and walk about twenty minutes down the beach to the point. This area is now a designated national marine park to protect the dazzling array of fish here and halt further coral damage. If you visit by boat, note that a $2 entrance fee is required, but tour operators often don't include this in the price they quote at the dock.

Playa Mirador

Blvd Kukulcán Km 22.5. For the true isolationist, this long, narrow beach on the mainland, dotted with a few palm trees, is usually deserted. Sea grass grows in patches in the shallow water, but the sand is kept very tidy and clean. Bring everything you need for the day, as there are no shops nearby, nor any services at the beach itself.

Parque Nizuc

Blvd Kukulcán Km 23 ☎998/881-3030, ☞www.parquenizuc.com. Daily: May–October 10am–6pm; Nov–April 10am–5.30pm. $25, kids $19. The centrepiece of this eighteen-acre beachfront complex is a Wet' n Wild water park, filled with long, looping slides, a wave pool and a lazy river. Appealing to adrenaline fans is a thrill ride on the Sho-tover Jet high-speed boat, and visitors can also swim with dolphins, sharks or rays in a small fenced area of the sea. Nothing's very state of the art, but it's a good place to wear the kids out. Note that inner tubes and snorkel gear cost extra – but are necessary if you want to enjoy the water park fully.

Accommodation

Ambiance Villas at Kin-Ha

Blvd Kukulcán Km 8 ☎998/883-1100, ☞www.ambiancevillas.com. A hands-off hotel that feels more like an apartment complex. The big, tastefully furnished double-bed rooms ($145), studios with kitchenettes ($175) or full suites with one, two or three bed-rooms (all redone in the past few years) are especially good deals for families or groups. Every room has a terrace or balcony, and the beach is fantas-tically deep and scenic – only the one next door, at *El Presi-dente* (see p.58), is better.

Aquamarina Beach Hotel

Blvd Kukulcán Km 3.5 ☎998/849-4606, ☞www.aquamarina-beach. com.mx. Relatively small and good-value resort with all the trappings of a larger all-inclusive such as a pool, volleyball, mini-ature golf and thrice-weekly theme parties, but with a less hectic feel. The beach is a little skimpy, but all rooms have balconies, and some have kitch-enettes, for those who choose a European plan (room-only) rather than an all-inclusive package. Doubles from $120 (EP) or $180 (all-inclusive).

Aristos

Blvd Kukulcán Km 19.5 ☎998/885-3333, ☞www.aristoshotels.com. At the southern end of the strip and far removed from the action, *Aristos* has a rather austere feel, with expanses of treeless con-crete, but the large rooms do come with marble floors and bathtubs, and the beach here is quite nice. European bargain-seekers dominate the guest register. Doubles from $100.

Avalon Baccará

Blvd Kukulcán Km 11.5 ☎800/713-8170 in Mexico, or in the US on 800/261-5014, ☞www .avalonvacations.com. Carved-wood furniture and colourful mosaics distinguish this smaller hotel with 27 individually styled rooms and suites. Nice touches like free snacks and tequila before dinner give the place a more personal feel. This hotel was the setting for MTV's *The Real Cancun*, but the usual clientele is older and more business-oriented than their onscreen counterparts. Standard rooms with king-size beds from $155.

Dreams Cancun

Punta Cancún ☎998/848-7000, ☞www.dreamsresorts.com. This landmark modern hotel built in 1975 (see p.54) is now a deluxe family resort with a strong sense of contemporary Mexican style. Hip parents will appreciate the sleek modern furniture and abstract art and the two beaches, while children can frolic in the protected lagoon. Quality restaurants and no tacky wristbands add to the sophisticated feel. All-inclusive rack rates start at $265 per person; lower promotional rates are usually available.

Grand Royal Lagoon

C Quetzal 8-A ☎998/883-1270, ☜www.grlagoon.com. Just 36 rooms make up this family-owned hotel – they're small but spotless, with cheerful lavender and white decor, set around an equally small pool. A few studio rooms have kitchenettes. This is the least you can pay in the *zona hotelera*, and it's conveniently close to the main boulevard. Doubles from $70.

Imperial Laguna

C Quetzal 11 ☎998/883-4270, ☜www.hotelimperialcancun.com. The best value of the lagoon-facing hotels, particularly in the off-season, when prices can drop by

more than half, offering 61 very big rooms with kitchens and balconies. The grounds also hold a pretty pool, a small garden and a restaurant with a great view over the water and mangroves. Doubles from $85.

Le Meridien

Blvd Kukulcán Km 14 ☎998/881-2200, ☜www.meridiencancun.com.mx. This French-run luxury hotel is relatively understated compared to the neighbouring *Ritz-Carlton Cancún*, with just 213 tastefully furnished rooms, rooftop tennis courts and three pools of different temperatures. The hotel's Spa del Mar is the best in Cancún, with hydrotherapy treatments, body wraps and massages from $60 (open to non-guests). Doubles from $350.

El Presidente Inter-Continental

Blvd Kukulcán Km 8 ☎998/848-8700, ☜www.inter-continental.com. One of the *zona's* oldest hotels, done in the same minimalist style as *Dreams Cancun*, although the 306 rooms are not quite as

▼EL PUEBLITO

distinctive as the lobby. More important, however, is what lies just beyond the hotel's back doors: a great, deep beach dotted with palm trees, facing placid bay waters. Doubles from $150.

El Pueblito

Blvd Kukulcán Km 18 ☎998/881-8800, ⊛www.pueblitohotels.com. A rare find in Cancún in that it feels more Mexican than American, with big, colourful tile-floor rooms in rustic-looking stucco buildings, an elaborate array of pools and a nice patch of beach. Service is exceptionally friendly, and reasonable rates include all food and drink – though note that the low prices make it appealing to spring-breakers in late March and April. A pretty white-stucco chapel is set aside for weddings. All-inclusive rates from $130 per person.

Ritz-Carlton Cancún

Retorno del Rey 36, off Blvd Kukulcán Km 14 ☎998/881-0808, ⊛www .ritzcarlton.com. The last word in luxury in Cancún, though with utterly no regard for its Mexican location. The posh chandeliers, tapestries and deep carpeting even seem a bit preposterous, as though transported intact from some fictional French villa to the tropics. Food and service, particularly for drinks on the 1.2-kilometre-long beach, are of course up to the highest international standards. Doubles from $429.

Sheraton Cancún Resort & Towers

Blvd Kukulcán Km 12 ☎998/891-4400, ⊛www.sheraton.com/cancun. The *Sheraton* is an older resort that's a bit nondescript in its architecture, but its beach is exceptionally beautiful and huge

– almost a kilometre long – and the pools are large; there's also a mini-golf course and lighted tennis courts. The club tower rooms are a big step up from the main hotel section, and worth the extra money; in the main building, the suites with palatial terraces ($419) are the best rooms; the rest are perfectly comfortable and often very affordable. Guests may also use the more glamorous facilities at the *Westin*. Doubles from $259.

Suites Girasol

Blvd Kukulcán Km 9.5 ☎998/883-5045. A deal for the independent traveller, this converted condo high-rise offers few frills but good-value basic amenities. The somewhat shabby entry and public areas don't look promising, but the rooms are surprisingly large and clean, and all have kitchenettes. The pool has also gotten a touch-up, and the beach out front is gorgeous. Doubles from $100.

Suites Sina

C Quetzal 33 ☎998/883-1017, ⊛www.cancunsinasuites.com.mx. Personable staff preside over 33 vast suites, each with either one ($100) or two bedrooms ($140), a sofa bed in the living room and a full kitchen and dining room, though some sport a not-so-cheerful brown decorating scheme. The pool is huge, and a sundeck overlooks the lagoon.

Villas Manglar

Blvd Kukulcán Km 20 ☎998/885-1808, ⊛www.villasmanglar.com. A blink-and-you'll-miss-it villa hidden in the wilds of the lagoon-side mangroves. You can lounge by the small pool, but the main draw is the sport-fishing tours ($375 per day) run by the experienced owners. If you have a group, ask for the connecting suites; the second-storey rooms get better light. Continental breakfast included. Doubles from $120.

Villas Tacul

Blvd Kukulcán Km 5.5 ☎998/883-0000, ⊛www.villastacul.com.mx. A smaller resort that's refreshingly glitz-free and gives visitors plenty of space to relax: individual villas, each containing two or three private rooms, are scattered over twelve beautifully landscaped acres, with gardens, tennis courts and a pool. Big rocks break up the beach, which is generally a pretty, calm stretch. The decor is a little old-fashioned, with lots of heavy wood, but you'd pay significantly more for trendier rooms on the same grounds. Doubles from $220.

▼VILLAS TACUL

Westin Resort & Spa Cancún

Blvd Kukulcán Km 20 ☎998/848-7400, ⊛www.westin.com. The striking, minimalist hotel has some luxurious touches: decadent pillow-top beds, deluxe showers and impressive views off the southern point and over the small lagoon nestled here. Standard rooms actually feel a bit cozier than the austere, all-white ones in the club tower. An additional west-facing beach and pool on the lagoon get afternoon sun. The place often hosts big conventions and events and is somewhat isolated, but a free shuttle runs up to the *Sheraton*, where guests may use the facilities. Doubles from $299.

Shops

Coral Negro

Blvd Kukulcán Km 9 ☎998/883-0758. Even as sections of the hotel zone are getting up-to-the-minute makeovers, this maze-like craft market remains a haven for useless knick-knacks, where you'll find not only an overwhelming selection of inexpensive sandals, silver bracelets and Mexican blankets, but also giant sombreros, tasteless T-shirts, refrigerator magnets, lewd ceramic figurines and other timeless souvenirs of Cancún's tackier side.

La Isla Shopping Village

Blvd Kukulcán Km 12 ☎998/883-5025, ⊛www.laislacancun.com.mx. The best of the *zona hotelera*'s malls, offering all the big international brands from Bulgari to Zara, as well as less familiar names like Zingara (sharp swimwear from Uruguay), Cocot & Nuit lingerie and Los Castillo jewellers. Non-shoppers will be kept well

▲LA ISLA SHOPPING VILLAGE

occupied, with the dual-purpose Hippo's Internet bar and music store, a cinema, several good restaurants and bars and an interactive aquarium (somewhat over-priced at $13; kids $9).

Plaza Caracol

Blvd Kukulcán Km 8.5 ⓦwww .plazacaracol.com. Vast indoor mall with plenty of standard-issue souvenirs, but a few good shops too. Keep an eye out for Mosaïqe, which stocks dressy clothing, natural-stone jewellery, feather boas and silk slippers, all organized by colour; Xaman-Ek gallery, representing established local artists and craftspeople; and Majoli, dealing in the eco look: natural-fibre clothing in crisp designs.

Plaza Kukulcán

Blvd Kukulcán Km 13 ⓦwww .kukulcanplaza.com. After a make-over in 2004, this mall has more luxury boutiques than before and a slightly nicer ambiance. A very large art gallery (Galería Kukulcán, in the north section) has a few eye-catching original works by Cancún artists, and a tobacconist on the ground floor deals in Cuban cigars. Also

check out La Ruta de las Indias, which specializes in Conquest chic: replica swords, armour and nautical trappings.

Cafés

100% Natural

Plaza Kukulcán, Blvd Kukulcán Km 13; Plaza Terramar, Blvd Kukulcán Km 8.4 ☏998/883-3636. A bit pricey, but the place to go for a health-food hit, such as a sandwich bursting with fresh veggies and sprouts (about $6), a hearty smoothie ($2.50) or a slab of grilled nopal (cactus paddle) – a satisfying meat substitute.

Ty-Coz

Blvd Kukulcán Km 7 and Blvd Kukulcán Km 7.7. A sandwich shop where French and Mexican tastes mix: the surprisingly large *baguette económico* ($1.25) of ham and cheese is served warm, slath-ered with garlic-herb mayo and studded with pickled jalapeños; smoky *chipotles* are optional. Excellent coffee and croissants for breakfast too. The small storefront at Km 7.7 closes around 6pm; the other, larger café, is open a little later.

Restaurants

La Casa de las Margaritas

La Isla Shopping Village, Blvd Kukulcán Km 12 ☎998/883-3222. Upscale Mexican restaurant that serves savoury regional specialities (*tlayudas*, Oaxacan corn cakes with assorted toppings, $9; hogfish with *cuitlacoche*, $18) and isn't quite as over-decorated as some, though the waiters are still done up in theatrical costumes and carry drinks on their heads. Live musicians perform assorted folk classics but don't dominate the room. The Sunday buffet ($13) is a very good deal.

Casa Rolandi

Plaza Caracol, Blvd Kukulcán Km 8.5 ☎998/831-1817, ⊛www.rolandi.com. This Cancún fixture since 1981 serves northern Italian specialities, many done in a wood-burning oven, presented in a candlelit, white-tablecloth setting. Expensive (mains range from pastas at $12 up to hefty steaks at $30) but good for a romantic splurge.

Checándole

Plaza Flamingo, Blvd Kukulcán Km 11 ☎998/885-1302. A local fast-food mini-chain with fresh-made Mexican staples – one of the few spots for satisfying, inexpensive local grub in the *zona hotelera*, though the setting is a mall food court. Taco plates start at $4, while full lunches are $6.50 and up.

La Destilería

Blvd Kukulcán Km 12.5 ☎998/885-1087. The food at this lagoon-side theme restaurant – stills stand in the dining room, and waiters give guided tours of the tequila-making process – is tasty, varied and not terribly expensive ($6.50 for *chalupas*, $14 for fish dishes). The real draw, however, is the hundred-plus kinds of tequila, available in tasting flights.

Dolcemente Pompei

Pez Volador 7, near Blvd Kukulcán Km 5 ☎998/849-4006. A rare casual restaurant that caters to Mexican families and residents in the *zona hotelera*, serving mammoth

▼ DOLCEMENTE POMPEI

portions of high-quality Italian food, from handmade pastas ($9 and up) to gelato to espresso with sambuca. A little hard to find because it's not affiliated with a mall or hotel: turn north in front of the giant Mexican flag.

El Galeón del Caribe

Blvd Kukulcán Km 19.2, across from the Club Solaris resort. A very rustic restaurant – more like a campsite – down the hill off the lagoon side of the road, where fresh-caught fish is grilled over wood fires or served up in ceviches, for $10 or less. Just north of bus stop #11, look for a small pull-off and stairs leading down to the water, and get your order in before dusk – there's not enough electricity to keep the place open after the sun sets.

Hanaichi

Plaza El Parián, Blvd Kukulcán Km 8.7 ☎998/883-2804. At this sparkling little sushi joint, Mexican waiters speak to the Japanese business clientele in their own language, while serving them quite decent sashimi ($2 per piece), maki rolls ($6.50–9) and other standards, such as beef *teppanyaki* ($16).

JC Capitán

Blvd Kukulcán Km 19.6. Fresh seafood is served up at this wooden pier jutting into the lagoon. It's more upscale than its neighbour *El Galeón*, and open past sunset, making it a mellow place for an evening drink and a shrimp taco or two ($1.20), if not the full "garlicky combo" platter ($18).

▲HANAICHI

El Rincón Yucateco

Plaza Maya Fair, Blvd Kukulcán Km 8.3. New branch of a downtown stalwart (see p.76), offering big, reasonably priced helpings of peninsula standards, such as crispy *panuchos* ($4.50 for four), light *sopa de lima* ($3.50) and *brazo de reina* ($5), a hearty tamale-like dish. A small taco place 100m east is run by the same people and is equally tasty and affordable.

Río Nizúc

Blvd Kukulcán near Km 22. Hidden among the mangroves at the south end of the lagoon, where dive boats and jet skiers head out to the open sea, is this cheap seafood specialist. Ceviches ($6) and *tikin-xic* (fish baked in banana leaves with *achiote*, $6) are popular with locals, who gather on weekends to watch the boats whiz by.

PLACES

Cancún's zona hotelera

Bars

Hard Rock Café

Plaza Forum by the Sea, Blvd Kukulcán Km 9 ☎998/881-8120, ⊛www .hardrock.com. The usual *Hard Rock* style – loud and packed with college kids eating cheese fries – is somewhat alleviated by a big back deck on the beach, with lounge chairs and drink service. At night, it offers live rock with no cover.

Lobby Bar at the Ritz-Carlton

Retorno del Rey 36, near Blvd Kukulcán Km 14 ☎998/881-0808, ⊛www .ritzcarlton.com. Soak up the ersatz French-château feel in the over-stuffed chairs, while listening to the tinkling piano. The only giveaways you're in Cancún: the sea view and the tequila menu. Classic cocktails start at $12.

La Madonna

La Isla Shopping Village, Blvd Kuku-lcán Km 12 ☎998/883-4837. A giant reproduction of the *Mona Lisa* presides over the candlelit nooks; the second-floor balcony seats are particularly good romantic hideaways. Wash down fondue and other Italian-Swiss dishes with one of 150 types of martinis (very loosely defined, obviously).

Pat O'Brien's

Plaza Flamingo, Blvd Kukulcán Km 11. Live rock, blues and jazz are the main attractions in a larger-than-life version of the famous New Orleans establishment. Three rooms pack in the ready-to-dance crowds: a piano bar, a video lounge and an outdoor patio.

Señor Frog's

Blvd Kukulcán Km 9.5 ☎998/883-1092, ⊛www.senorfrogs.com. Practically synonymous with the name Cancún, the *Frog's* is the first stop off the plane for the spring-break hordes. Go for live reggae or karaoke, or just an anthropological experience.

Trágara

Blvd Kukulcán Km 15.6 ☎998/885-0267, ⊛www.lagunagrill.com.mx. Velvet couches, moody lighting, numerous aquariums and mosaic trim on every surface set a super-cool mood in this breezy lagoon-front lounge – the perfect spot for a sunset drink and a snack from the Asian-fusion finger-food menu.

▼SEÑOR FROG'S

Clubs

Azúcar

At Dreams Cancun, Punta Cancún ⊕998/848-7000. Closed Sun. Popular, classy Caribbean club with a ten-piece band that gets the well-dressed crowd grooving to salsa and merengue. Cover $8; call to reserve a table, as the place can get packed.

Batacha

At Miramar Misión, Blvd Kukulcán 9.7 ⊕998/883-1755. Closed Mon. $5. This small salsa club recently got a makeover, but its appeal remains the same – a hot, sweaty little room, that's perhaps the most fun place to dance to Caribbean music in Cancún.

La Boom

Blvd Kukulcán Km 3.5, across from El Embarcadero ⊕998/849-7587, ⊛www .laboom.com.mx. The only place in the city that begins to approach Ibiza-style decadence, with international house hits on the sound system (occasionally spun by celeb DJs) and an open-air chill-out space. No cover charge on Mon; $25 open bar on Tues; otherwise, entry is usually $15.

Bulldog Café

At the Krystal hotel, Blvd Kukulcán 9 ⊕998/848-9851, ⊛www.bulldogcafe .com. Somewhat generic spring-breakers' party spot (complete with a "VIP hot tub"), but it does host touring Mexican rock and pop legends such as Café Tacuba and Molotov. Cover on non-concert nights is usually $15, or $28 for open bar.

The City

Blvd Kukulcán Km 9 ⊕998/848-8380, ⊛www.thecitycancun.com. This 24-hour club is a beach party by day (the pool area has a wave machine and a water slide) and a high-tech disco with a mesmerizing laser show by night. During spring break, MTV sets up shop here and the hip-hop and pop stars du jour dominate the bill; at other times, European DJs man the decks.

Coco Bongo

Plaza Forum by the Sea, Blvd Kukulcán Km 9 ⊕998/883-0592, ⊛www .cocobongo.com.mx. Vast state-of-the-art rock and pop disco popular with US college kids, with a hyper-stimulating floor show involving trapeze acts, Madonna impersonators and stunt bartenders. Cover charge at weekends only.

Glazz

La Isla Shopping Village, Blvd Kukulcán Km 12 ⊕998/883-1881, ⊛www.glazz .com.mx. Beautifully designed

▼LA BOOM

restaurant-lounge-club space. The lounge offers gigantic cocktails, lots of pillow-filled nooks, and hookahs; the separate club area, all done up in black and white, is relatively small, and can get packed after midnight.

G-Spot

Blvd Kukulcán Km 10.5 ☎998/883-2180, ◉www.gspotdisco.com. The scene is young and the soundtrack heavy on trance at this funky floating club, opened in late 2004. The semi-open space, filled with plants and curvy, free-form furniture, is refreshingly small compared to the mega-clubs at Punta Cancún. Cover is $15.

Over 30 Club

Blvd Kukulcán Km 10.5 ☎998/892-0060. Hardly a less glamorous name could be imagined, but the atmosphere is indeed fun for the intended age bracket, with a live band doing covers of Sixties, Seventies and Eighties hits. No cover charge, and two-for-one beers get everyone dancing.

The Royal Bandstand

Blvd Kukulcán Km 13.5 ☎998/848-8220. A somewhat cheesy floor show and MC set an odd tone, but the big band plays a wide variety of music, making this supper club a pleasant enough place to dance for those who don't want to deal with 20-year-olds at the big clubs. It's also inexpensive: no cover, just a $7.50 drink minimum per person.

Shows and dinner cruises

Ballet Folklórico Nacional de México

At the convention centre, Blvd Kukulcán Km 8.8 ☎998/983-0199. Buffet dinner nightly at 7pm followed by the colourful, verging-on-campy traditional dance of this world-renowned troupe. Tickets cost around $40 including dinner.

Captain Hook

El Embarcadero, Blvd Kukulcán Km 4 ☎998/883-3736, ◉www.captainhook .com. Two replica Spanish galleons – modernized with a/c, nice restrooms and slick sound systems – set sail into the bay every night at 7pm, carrying 350 passengers, swashbuckling pirates, booze, and lobster and steak for all. Midway through the buffet dinner, there's a full-scale battle between the ships. You'll either love it as bizarre dinner theatre, or steer well clear. Tickets cost $60, or $70 for surf-and-turf; half-price for kids.

Teatro de Cancún

El Embarcadero, Blvd Kukulcán Km 4 ☎998/849-4848. This small modern theatre hosts the occasional touristy Caribbean song-and-dance extravaganza (pricey and more than a bit silly), but big-name Cuban bands, local theatre productions and the city's chamber orchestra often squeeze onto the bill; call for the schedule.

Downtown Cancún

Downtown Cancún is the "real world" counterpart to the *zona hotelera* vacation fantasy, a booming thirty-year-old city that's home to more than half a million people. The locals are young, cosmopolitan and diverse, having moved here from all over Mexico, as well as other parts of Latin America, to make their fortunes in tourism. Avenida Tulum serves as the principal artery, and nightlife centres on Avenida Yaxchilán and, more casually, El Crucero. Actual sights are few, and there's little history to soak up, but an evening stroll through the winding neighbourhood streets could take you past an Oaxacan artisans' fair, a public art show, a ska band playing for a crowd of teen punks, or simply families chatting on their porches. Great inexpensive restaurants, both regional Mexican and international, are plentiful, and staying at one of the reasonably priced hotels here doesn't mean sacrificing the beach, as buses run every few minutes to the *zona hotelera*.

Parque de las Palapas

C Margaritas. The recreational heart of downtown Cancún is unassuming Parque de las Palapas, named for the thatch-roof food stalls that used to surround it. The stalls are now more permanent, and the place to go for inexpensive snacks after dark: a couple of clusters of food stalls serve up quesadillas, *huaraches* and tacos with a fabulous array of toppings. The whole park is a little short on greenery – instead, the large bandstand is the focus, especially on weekend evenings, when there are live music or dance performances. On the east side of the park is a Ferris wheel and other kiddie rides, which add to the festive atmosphere. La Parroquia de Cristo Rey, a striking modern semi-open church (Mass five times on Sun) sits on the northeast corner. Also worth checking out are the four smaller parks just to the north

▼ DUB CAFÉ

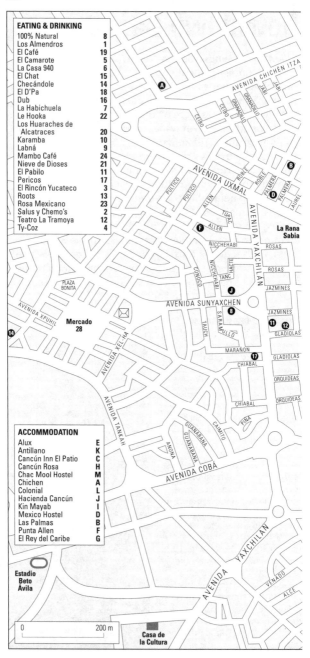

EATING & DRINKING

100% Natural	8
Los Almendros	1
El Café	19
El Camarote	5
La Casa 940	6
El Chat	15
Checándole	14
El D'Pa	18
Dub	16
La Habichuela	7
Le Hooka	22
Los Huaraches de Alcatraces	20
Karamba	10
Labná	9
Mambo Café	24
Nieve de Dioses	21
El Pabilo	11
Pericos	17
El Rincón Yucateco	3
Roots	13
Rosa Mexicano	23
Salus y Chemo's	2
Teatro La Tramoya	12
Ty-Coz	4

ACCOMMODATION

Alux	E
Antillano	K
Cancún Inn El Patio	C
Cancún Rosa	H
Chac Mool Hostel	M
Chichen	A
Colonial	L
Hacienda Cancún	J
Kin Mayab	I
Mexico Hostel	D
Las Palmas	B
Punta Allen	F
El Rey del Caribe	G

La Rana Sabia

AVENIDA CHICHÉN ITZÁ
JABÍ
JABÍ
GRANADILLO
GRANADILLO
CEIBO

AVENIDA UXMAL
ROBLE
ROBLE
PALMERA
PALMERA
LAUREL

PÚLTICO
PÚLTICO
ALLEN
TUPAC
ALLEN

AVENIDA YAXCHILÁN

NICCHEHABÍ
ROSAS
ROSAS

NICCHEHABÍ
TANC
JAZMINES
JAZMINES

CÚNICO

AVENIDA SUNYAXCHEN
SARAMULLO
TAUCH
GLADIOLAS
GLADIOLAS

MARAÑON
CHIABAL
ORQUIDEAS
ORQUIDEAS

PLAZA BONITA

AVENIDA XPUHIL

Mercado 28

CHIABAL
PIÑA

AVENIDA KELHA

GUANABANA
GUANABANA
CAIMITO
ANONA

AVENIDA TANKAH

AVENIDA COBÁ

AVENIDA YAXCHILÁN
VENADO
ALCE

Estadio Beto Ávila

0   200 m

Casa de la Cultura

El Crucero

N

Mercado 23

CEDRO
CEDRO
FLAMBOYAN
FLAMBOYAN
CHACA
CHACA
PINO

CIRICOTE
LAUREL
MARGARITAS
MARGARITAS
JAZMINES
AZUCENAS
TULIPANES
TULIPANES
CLAVELES
CLAVELES
CRISANTEMOS
CRISANTEMOS
ALCATRACES
ALCATRACES

AVENIDA TULUM

AVENIDA J. C. NADER

AVENIDA DE LA TORRE

GRANADA
NARANJA
GRANADA
NARANJA
DURAZNO
CEREZA
DURAZNO
CEREZA
TORONJA
LIMA

AVENIDA UXMAL

RUBIA
ROBALO
MERO
MERO

BARRACUDA
CAZON
CAZON
PARGO
PARGO
CHERNA
CHERNA

AVENIDA J. C. NADER

HUACHINANGO
MOJARRA
MOJARRA

ROBALO
JUREL

SIERRA
ROBALO

AVENIDA BONAMPAK

Bus Station

Parque de
las Palapas

Ayuntamiento
i
Bank
Fama

Ki-Huic
Flea
Market

AVENIDA COBÁ

AVENIDA COBÁ

AVENIDA COBÁ

XCARET
RENO
RENO
JALEB
JALEB
TEJON
TEJON
PECARI
PECARI
LIEBRE

VENDO
ALCE

AVENIDA TULUM

LLUVIA
AGUA
AGUA
VIENTO

American
Express

BRISA
NUBE
NUBE
CIELO
CIELO

AVENIDA BONAMPAK

Plaza de Toros

Visiting downtown Cancún

To reach downtown Cancún from the airport, the least expensive option is the half-hourly Riviera bus ($1.50) that runs between 5.30am and midnight to the **bus** station. Tickets are available from booths just beyond customs; the bus itself departs from the south end of the main terminal. A **taxi** ride costs around $20.

The helpful **tourist office** is inside the city hall at Avenida Tulum 26 (daily 9am–8pm, ☎998/884-8073).

and south, which often host art shows and smaller bands.

Avenida Yaxchilán

Downtown Cancún's nightlife is concentrated in a three-block strip along Avenida Yaxchilán between avenidas Sunyaxchén and Uxmal. In marked contrast to the club scene in the hotel zone, the atmosphere here is calmer and the entertainment in the open-terrace bars and restaurants is limited to TVs, karaoke and roving *trovadores*, who can be hired for a romantic serenade at the corner of Calle Tanchacte. The strip comes to life after sundown, and though a few touts push menus at tourists, the clientele is mostly Mexican.

El Crucero

Av Lopez Portillo at Av Tulum. Once Cancún's geographic centre and meeting point, El Crucero (simply "the intersection") has become a busy convergence of four-lane streets, though it remains a popular night-time hangout. The southwest corner in particular is a throng of activity; families and teenagers lounge around, while *elote* vendors (selling boiled corn on the cob, slathered in mayo, crumbly cheese, lime and chile) and a *Domino's Pizza* are equally mobbed. Head a little bit west on Avenida Lopez Portillo and you'll reach a cluster of market stalls that cater solely to locals. Although not much on offer – such as meat smokers, underwear

and fly-swatters – will tempt a tourist, it's that rare shopping area where you stroll free from the "Hey, *amigo*!" sales push.

Plaza de Toros

Av Bonampak at Av Sayil ☎998/884-8248. Wed 3.30pm. $30. This bullring is the most frequently used in Mexico, hosting a full roster of bullfights every week of the year. The *corrida* is now preceded by an hour of shameless tourist spectacle, a parade of colourful skirts and blaring mariachi music. But the small covered arena has a certain dusty ambiance, and it's the only place in the area with a regular *corrida*; otherwise, you'll have to wait for a town fiesta somewhere inland. The ring's outer walls are lined with lively traditional cantinas – generous with snacks to accompany your drinks, though not particularly welcoming to women – as well as *El Timón de Cancún*, a longstanding seafood specialist recently relocated to this spot.

Casa de la Cultura

Av Prolongación Yaxchilán ☎998/884-8364. The city's flourishing cultural centre hosts lectures, films and musical performances – usually all free – as well as shows by local artists, some of whom are quite talented. If you're interested in purchasing original art, the selection and prices here are far better than at the few galleries in the malls in the hotel zone. The centre's events are listed in the free monthly listings flyer *Entérate Cancún*, which can be picked up at *La Rana Sabía* bookshop and some cafés around town.

Estadio Beto Ávila

Av Xcaret west of Av Tulum. Root for the local major-league team, the Langosteros, alongside a mob of dedicated but well-mannered fans at the city's somewhat tumbledown main baseball field. Check *Entérate Cancún* for schedules – there are usually eight or nine evening games here per month during the season, which runs from March to June. Bleacher seats are $2, and the best seats in the house are only $8; they're rarely sold out.

Accommodation

Alux

Av Uxmal 21 ☎998/884-6613, ⊛www .hotelalux.com.mx. Popular, good-value hotel, if a little dated with its mirror-clad decor. The small-ish rooms have a/c, TV and telephone; a sidewalk café and a travel agency next door are added conveniences. Doubles from $30.

Antillano

C Claveles 1 at Av Tulum ☎998/884-1532, ⊛www.hotelantillano.com. A notch above *Kin Mayab* (see

p.72), with big, clean rooms with tile floors, very effective a/c, a pool and a travel agency. Continental breakfast included. Doubles from $70.

Cancún Inn El Patio

Av Bonampak 51 ☎998/884-3500, ⊛www.cancuninn.com. A hands-off staff and a location in a quiet residential neighbourhood make this small hotel feel more like a private apartment complex – though it's still an easy walk to downtown. The thirteen rooms are simple but comfortable, and ring a quiet garden courtyard. Doubles from $45.

Cancún Rosa

C Margaritas 2 ☎998/884-0623. Old-fashioned hotel with velvet sofas and plastic flowers in the lobby, and a pool and overgrown garden out back. A/c is standard in all the rooms, which can be a little dark; a huge one on the second floor with four beds ($60) is ideal for groups or families. Doubles from $50.

Chac Mool Hostel

C Gladiolas 18 ☎998/887-5873, ⊛chacmoolhostels@hotmail.com. Opened in 2004, this tidy hostel has small four-bed dorms ($10 per person) as well as a few private rooms, and the option

▼ CHAC MOOL HOSTEL

of a/c. The cool rooftop lounge, with a pretty view over El Parque de las Palapas, serves $1 drinks (to non-guests too). Free Internet access is another perk.

Chichen

C 2 121 off Av Chichén ☎ 998/884-4440 ⓔ hotelchichen@prodigy.net.mx. A less-visited motel with well-appointed rooms with a/c, cable TV and fridges. It's a bit out of the centre, but handy if travelling by car – you're away from the worst traffic, and there's secure parking in the courtyard. Doubles from $40.

Colonial

C Tulipanes 22 ☎ & ⓕ 998/884-1535. Fifty well-lit, simple rooms are simple and modern, with TV and a choice of a/c or fan.

▼EL REY DEL CARIBE HOTEL

But the place still has a little character, thanks to a small central courtyard. A decent bargain, in a prime location not far from the bus station and in the middle of downtown's liveliest neighbourhood. Doubles from $30.

Hacienda Cancún

Av Sunyaxchén 39 ☎ 998/884-3672, ⓕ 884-1208. Not to be confused with the pricier, business-oriented *Radisson Hacienda Cancún*, this smaller hotel, built in an old mansion style, offers good value in a quiet location. All rooms have a/c and TV, and there's a big pool, a pretty garden and a basic café. Doubles from $45.

Kin Mayab

Av Tulum 75, at Av Uxmal ☎ 998/884-2999, ⓦ www.hotelkinmayab.com. Centrally located, clean and secure, it's the best hotel in its class – be sure to book ahead. Rooms, with a fan or a/c, are very comfortable, though try to get one in the back section, by the pool and away from the street noise. Doubles from $62.

Mexico Hostel

C Palmera 30, at Av Uxmal ☎ 998/887-0191, ⓦ www.mexicohostels.com. The oldest and most popular Cancún hostel, with several dorm rooms and a rooftop terrace where you can hang a hammock. Internet access, bike rental and laundry are available too. Dorm beds from $9.50.

Las Palmas

C Palmeras 43 ☎ 998/884-2513, ⓔ hotelpalmascancun@hotmail.com. This small family-run hostel caters as much to Mexican workers as to backpackers, so there's less of a party atmosphere. Its main draw are clean and cheap ($10) dorm beds in big rooms with a/c, a few huge private rooms (starting at $30), and there's a communal kitchen too. Continental breakfast included.

Punta Allen

C Punta Allen 8 ☎998/884-0225, ⓦwww.puntaallen.da.ru. Small but spotless rooms, all with a/c, in a guesthouse full of kitschy, time-warp furnishings. Avenida Yaxchilán is nearby, but the block itself is very quiet. Doubles from $32, with continental breakfast included.

El Rey del Caribe

Av Uxmal 24, at Av Nader ☎998/884-2028, ⓦwww.reycaribe.com. Sunny yellow rooms with kitchenettes, plus a pool and spa services at this mellow hacienda-style hotel – the only one in Cancún with an active ecological sensibility, with composting and solar water heaters. Good discounts in the low season. Doubles from $60.

Shops

Fama

Av Tulum between C Tulipanes and C Claveles. From the street, this looks like a typical souvenir shop, but in the back is a decent collection of travel guides and other English-language books, for those starving for a good read.

Ki-Huic

Av Tulum north of Av Cobá. An unabashed tourist trap, this so-called "flea market" is packed to the rafters with T-shirts and cheap knick-knacks. It's a lot of the same average-quality stuff as in the Coral Negro market (see p.60), but doesn't require a trip to the hotel zone – and it's marginally cheaper.

▲ KI-HUIC

Mercado 23

Off Av Tulum at C Cedro. Daily 7am–4pm. This small maze of stalls has the flavour of a village market, complete with butchers, vegetable sellers with stacks of local greens and miniature mangoes, and herbalists offering cure-alls in bulk from burlap bags. Don't miss the store packed wall-to-wall with piñatas, party favours and Mexican candies.

Mercado 28

Av Sunyaxchén at Av Xel-Há, behind the post office. Daily 7am–5pm. Formerly the city's main general market, this collection of open-air shops now stocks primarily tourist tat, catering to the busloads arriving to see a "real" Mexican *mercado*. Still, it's nowhere near as high-pressure and crowded as Ki-Huic, and a few traditional vendors remain, peddling wildly coloured sweets and the fresh *masa* that, when pressed and cooked, becomes corn tortillas. Two rows of food stalls, a sort of pan-Mexican food court, are especially worth perusing, with specialities from Monterrey, Mexico City, Guadalajara and elsewhere – and even one restaurant dedicated to dishes featuring *chaya* (a spinach-like plant that's a purported cure-all). This part of the market is particularly festive on weekend afternoons, when it's a popular destination for families.

Plaza Bonita

Av Sunyaxchén at Av Xel-Há, northwest corner of the block. Adjacent to Mercado 28, this pleasant shopping complex, built to resemble a colonial town, has a diverse range of stores, from herb sellers and juice shops to jewellers and clothing boutiques. A highlight is the branch of El Aguacate, the famed Mérida hammock-maker, where you can pick up a densely woven hammock for about $20. To be sure it's big enough, buy at least a *doble,* or, better still, a *matrimonial* if you can afford it.

La Rana Sabia

Av Uxmal 32, at C Margaritas ☎998/892-3627. Primarily a Spanish-language bookstore, *La Rana Sabia* also carries an eclectic stock of esoterica, philosophy, gay and lesbian titles. Pick up a copy of the listings flyer *Entérate Cancún* here.

Cafés

El Café

Av Nader 5, behind the city hall. This buzzing terrace is frequented by Cancún's journalists and writers, who come to enjoy the good coffee and *pan dulce*, along with simple, reasonably priced diner staples like steak and fries ($8) or Mexican standards such as *chilaquiles* for breakfast and *enchiladas de mole* for dinner.

El D'Pa

C Alcatraces at the southwest corner of El Parque de las Palapas. Closed Mon. Typical French crepes, both sweet and savoury ($3.50–7.50), and decent wine by the glass are served late afternoons and evenings. Choose a sidewalk table or inside among plush furniture – either way, it's very comfortable, and lively at night.

Dub

Av Nader at C Mero. Chilled-out hip café, usually with a DJ providing a live soundtrack. Ice

▼EL D'PA

cream, sandwiches and coffee are on the day menu, with wine and light snacks (*jamón serrano*, olives, salads) at night.

Nieve de Dioses

Av Nader behind the city hall. Tasty ice cream and sorbet, from extra-creamy *tres leches* (triple milk) to *coco con ginebre* (coconut with ginger), are the specialities here. Try spicing up fruit flavours with the chile-salt mixture set out on the counter.

El Pabilo

Av Yaxchilán 31, in the *Xbalamqué* hotel. Literary coffee shop (a *cafébrería* with very good cappuccino, espresso and snacks. The atmosphere is mellow and beatnik-cool, and at night there's usually live guitar music or readings.

Ty-Coz

Av Tulum behind the *Comercial Mexicana* ☏998/884-6060. Closed Sun. The deluxe main location of this French sandwich shop has more seating, longer hours (open till 11pm) and a slightly bigger menu than its hotel zone branches do. As there, the huge and delicious $1.25 *baguette económico* is perhaps the most enticing option. Also good for breakfast, with buttery pastries and strong coffee; pop into their patisserie in the alley if you just want a takeaway.

Restaurants

100% Natural

Av Sunyaxchén 26, at Av Yaxchilán. As the name implies, the menu at this largely vegetarian restaurant is decidedly wholesome, with fruit salads, yoghurt and granola, as well as Mexican dishes,

▲NIEVE DE DIOSES

seafood and veggie burgers. Breakfasts are especially nice: stick-to-your-ribs whole-wheat pancakes ($3.50), fruit shakes ($2.50) and inventive dishes like poached eggs over *nopal* leaves with spinach and an almond cream sauce ($4).

Los Almendros

Av Tulum 66. The original restaurant, in the small town of Ticul in the centre of the peninsula, boasts of inventing the emblematic Yucatecan spicy pork dish *poc-chuc*. This new Cancún branch is somewhat stiff, with bright lights and white tablecloths, but the food is hearty and reasonably priced, with main dishes like *cochinita pibil* (slow-cooked pork in banana leaves) for about $8. Nightly specials on Mon, Wed, Thurs and Sun are a good deal and a chance to try less common traditional specialities.

Checándole

Av Xpuhil 67. Closed Sun. The setting in this original restaurant is much homier than its branch in the *zona hotelera*, with a breezy terrace and none of the plastic food-court trappings. All the food is satisfying and fresh-tasting: taco plates start at $4; entrées like enchiladas are $6.50 and up, or choose the $4 set lunch.

La Habichuela

C Margaritas 25, in front of El Parque de las Palapas ☎998/884-3158. Long-established and very elegant restaurant set in a tranquil walled garden. The featured dish, the *cocobichuela* (half a coconut filled with lobster and shrimp in a curry sauce, accompanied by tropical fruits, $31), draws rave reviews, but simpler, and less expensive, concoctions are equally savoury. The sommelier is attentive and enthusiastic.

Los Huaraches de Alcatraces

C Alcatraces 31 (or enter on C Claveles). Closed Mon. This sparkling-clean cafeteria-style restaurant serves filling hot lunches – usually specialities from Guadalajara and Jalisco – for about $5 and snacks like *huaraches* and quesadillas ($2) with an array of fillings. It's all very fresh, and the staff is happy to explain the various dishes.

Labná

C Margaritas 29 ☎998/892-3056. The owners of *La Habichuela* next door have applied the same elegant flair to Yucatecan specialities here at *Labná*, such as *pan de cazón* (shredded shark meat layered in tortillas, $17), Valladolid-style spicy pork loin ($7) and even a soulful *lomo en Coca-Cola*, with slightly lower prices.

Pericos

Av Yaxchilán 61 ☎998/884-3152. What opened in 1974 as a four-table *lonchería* is now a phantasmagoria of strolling magicians, crooning mariachis, stilt-walkers and juggling barmen. The borderline surreal atmosphere is so over-the-top that even sceptical diners may get swept up in the audience participation. The food (steaks and enchiladas, $14–25) is tasty, if not novel.

El Rincón Yucateco

Av Uxmal 24. Closed Sun. Open since 1981, this stalwart specializes in simple Yucatecan cuisine such as *panuchos* ($4 for four) and *brazo de reina* ($5), washed down with cold beers. The busy street out front makes dining out on the terrace less than ideal, but the chummy staff make up for it.

Rosa Mexicano

C Claveles 4 ☎998/884-6313. This pretty tiled house with a garden is primarily a tourist destination, but the menu is well executed and relatively inexpensive – squid in tangy *escabeche* ($10) and *pollo almendrado* (chicken in a coriander-almond sauce, $9) are some of the pricier dishes.

Salus y Chemo's

C Chacá 46. Closed Mon. This quiet, pretty neighbourhood restaurant behind the bus station prepares a hearty *pozole* (spicy hominy stew), and the generous set lunch specials ($4.50) are a great deal.

Bars

El Camarote

In the *Plaza Kokai* hotel, Av Uxmal 26 ☎998/884-3218. At this nautical-theme bar, older local gentlemen play backgammon and cards on the front terrace. Inside is a small theatre furnished with captains' chairs and a stage – the live music ($3 cover, every night but Sun) tends toward sad ballads.

La Casa 940

C Margaritas near C Azucenas. Local ska and jam bands play for a mixed clientele of students and assorted bohemian types. If the band's not your thing, hang out on the front porch and sample some cheap seafood snacks to go with your beer.

El Chat

C Tulipanes opposite *Roots*. An Internet café by day, *El Chat* draws pool players and a young, rock-loving crowd in the evenings. If a live band isn't playing (usually for free), it's all Nirvana on the booming sound system.

Le Hooka

Av Nader behind the city hall. Open late, this slick Middle Eastern–theme lounge boasts international DJ beats and a big terrace with comfy couches that invite relaxation while mellowing out with a water pipe and sweet apple tobacco.

Clubs

Karamba

Av Tulum at C Azucenas @www .karambabar.com. Closed Mon. The biggest and busiest gay disco in town, in a breezy, open-sided spot with room for four hundred to dance to pounding house, salsa and the requisite gay anthems. Most nights see drag acts, strippers and go-go boys galore. Cover is rarely more than $5.

Mambo Café

Plaza Las Américas, Av Tulum south of Av Sayil ☎998/887-7894. Closed Mon & Tues. Cancún's biggest salsa club has a vast wood dance floor and elaborate jungle decor, complete with a water-fall. The crowd is young, but serious about salsa. Live bands – often touring acts from Cuba, the Dominican Republic and Puerto Rico – start around 11pm. No cover Wednesdays, otherwise about $5.

Roots

C Tulipanes 26 ☎998/884-2437, ©roots@cancun.com. Closed Sun & Mon. A funky, intimate jazz and blues club that's downtown Cancún's preeminent venue for live music, often hosting big-name touring musicians. Also serves dinner. Cover is $3 on Fri and Sat.

Teatro La Tramoya

C Gladiolas 8 ☎998/108-0503. Tap into the local arts scene at this intimate theatre and bar with live performances most nights of the week. Spanish-only stand-up comedy or cabaret usually fill the bill, with the occasional tango show.

Isla Mujeres

A hippie hangout in the 1970s, eight-kilometre-long **Isla Mujeres** still retains an air of bohemian languor, with wild-haired baby boomers passing on travel wisdom and tales to the next generation of backpackers. The place gets mobbed with day-trippers from Cancún – a fifteen-minute ferry ride to the southwest – and the streets of the island's compact and colourful main town are chockablock with T-shirts and trinkets. Underneath the tourist veneer, however, this tiny island is substantially mellower than the mainland, in a way that tends to draw people for long stays despite the lack of traditional attractions and wild nightlife. The chief daytime diversion is beach lounging, perhaps punctuated by a snorkel trip, or a bicycle tour down to the southern tip of the island and up the rugged Caribbean coast. By nightfall you'll want to be back under the palms on Playa Norte, the island's biggest beach and one of the few places along Mexico's eastern shoreline where you can enjoy a glowing sunset over the water, margarita in hand.

Isla Mujeres town

The island's population is spread between two villages. The larger one, on the northern end at Punta Norte, is what greets tourists when they get off the ferry, and what holds the majority of the hotels, restaurants and bars. But "larger" is only relative – half an hour is all that's required to take a turn around the sixteen or so square blocks of brightly painted houses. **Avenida Hidalgo** is the main drag, lined with tequila bars, crochet-bikini vendors and family-friendly restaurants. It's also the only source of after-dark entertainment, following sunset on the beach: simply wander down the music-filled street and see what strikes your

Visiting Isla Mujeres

Isla Mujeres is served primarily by two **ferry** companies, Mexico Waterjets and Ultramar (15min, half-hourly 5.30am–midnight). The latter service is preferable for its newer boats and more central location at Gran Puerto (🌐www.granpuerto.com .mx), 3km north of downtown Cancún and accessible by most city "Hoteles" buses heading north on Avenida Tulum; Mexico Waterjets boats leave from Puerto Juárez, 1km farther north. Additionally, **boats** run from the *zona hotelera* – El Embarcadero and Playa Tortugas are two piers – but prices start at about $15 per person, and the crossing takes longer.

 The **tourist office**, on Avenida Medina between calles Madero and Morelos (🌐www.isla-mujeres-mexico.com; Mon–Fri 8am–8pm) is nominally useful, though not much English is spoken.

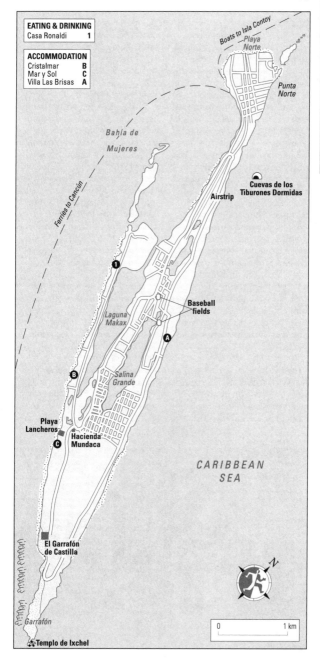

EATING & DRINKING
Casa Ronaldi   1

ACCOMMODATION
Cristalmar   B
Mar y Sol   C
Villa Las Brisas   A

Boats to Isla Contoy

Playa Norte

Punta Norte

Bahía de Mujeres

Ferries to Cancún

Cuevas de los Tiburones Dormidas

Airstrip

Laguna Makax

Baseball fields

Salina Grande

CARIBBEAN SEA

Playa Lancheros

Hacienda Mundaca

El Garrafón de Castilla

Garrafón

Templo de Ixchel

0   1 km

fancy. The southern end opens onto the central plaza, where vendors selling tamales, churros and *marquesitas* (crispy, cheese-filled crepes) set up shop in the evenings. One side of the square is dominated by a church that's the site of week-long festivities every December celebrating the legendary statue of the Virgin Mary that's on display inside.

The only other sight to speak of is the **town cemetery**, on Calle Mateos at Avenida Juárez, where you'll find the closing chapter of the saga of Fermín Antonio Mundaca (see p.82). Nestled between shiny new crypts is the pirate's weather-worn grave, half-buried in sand. It's empty, though: the lovelorn man died alone in Mérida. The grim engraving, allegedly carved by the gloomy Mundaca himself, reads, "Como eres, yo fui. Como soy, tu serás" ("As you are, I was. As I am, you will be").

Playa Norte

North end of the island. The primary draw on Isla Mujeres is this wide, relatively quiet beach stretching around the northern tip. It's the archetypal Caribbean beach, with soft, deep sand, plenty of palm trees and bathtub-warm water stretching out at knee height for nearly a kilometre in some spots. The western side, north of the ferry docks, is cluttered with fishing boats and ceviche stands; this is where *isleños* often swim and set up camp with the whole family on Sundays. At the northwestern tip, the beach party goes all week long, with a cluster of bars in perpetual happy hour; you can also rent kayaks for about $10 per hour. Proceeding across the northern side, the water gets shallower and the beach scene somewhat quieter. Close to the *Avalon Reef Club*, the all-inclusive resort on the promontory at the island's northeast corner, the water is a little deeper, with some rocky bits that are home to various species of tropical fish – making for easily accessible snorkelling here. The small bay in front of *Casa Maya* is particularly calm and a good spot for children to test the waters. All of the beach is public access, though you'll be expected to pay for chairs and umbrellas at

▼AVENIDA HIDALGO

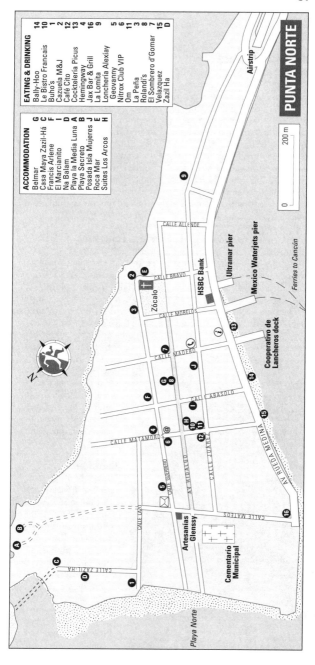

PUNTA NORTE

ACCOMMODATION

Belmar	G
Casa Maya Zazil-Há	C
Francis Arlene	F
El Marcianito	I
Na Balam	D
Playa la Media Luna	A
Playa Secreto	B
Posada Isla Mujeres	J
Roca Mar	E
Suites Los Arcos	H

EATING & DRINKING

Bally-Hoo	14
Le Bistro Francais	10
Buho's	1
Cazuela M&J	2
Café Cito	12
Cockteleria Picus	13
Hemingway	4
Jax Bar & Grill	16
La Lomita	9
Loncheria Alexiay	5
Nitrox Club VIP	6
Om	11
La Peña	3
Rolandi's	8
El Sombrero d'Gomar	7
Velazquez	15
Zazil Ha	D

the stretches in front of *María del Mar* and *Na Balam*.

Hacienda Mundaca

5km southeast from the ferries. Daily 9am–5pm. $1. In the centre of the island lie the barest remains of an old house and garden, to which scores of romantic (and quite untrue) legends are attached. In the mid-nineteenth century, Spaniard Fermín Antonio Mundaca, a reputed pirate (though more likely a trader of sugar and slaves) fell madly in love with a young lovely known as La Trigueña ("the brunette"). Mundaca built an enormous hacienda here and dedicated it to her, yet she ran off with someone her own age. Mundaca died alone and insane, and his glorious manse went to the dogs.

The buildings are hardly the draw (one small, blocky house

has been pieced together), but the entry gate is suitably gothic-looking, as the inscription "La Entrada de la Trigueña" can still barely be made out. A circular garden at the back of the property makes a pleasant and vaguely eerie picnic spot. Near the front and to the right of the main path is a zoo of the kind that makes you wonder whether the animals – sprawled sullenly on logs or sunken in pools – are actually alive. The stars are the spider monkeys, quick to pluck food and any other stray items from visitors' hands.

Playa Lancheros

5.5km south of town, just past Hacienda Mundaca. This small, palm-fringed beach is a nice alternative to Playa Norte, as the water is a bit deeper, and it's virtually deserted except around noon. That's when crowds arrive for lunch at the restaurant here, which produces some great rustic seafood. According to the battered sign over the wood-fire grills, ingredients in the fantastic *tikin-xic* fish are simply "*adobo*, salt, lime, vinegar . . . and love".

Garrafón

Southern tip of the island. Daily 9am–6.30pm. Adults $15, children $8. The small coral reef immediately off the southwestern tip of the island suffered serious damage from decades of unsupervised visitors until 1999, when the area came under stricter management as a family-fun nature park, with kayaking, restaurants and "snuba" set-ups (walk

▼GARDEN AT HACIENDA MUNDACA

under water while breathing through a long flexible tube). While much of the coral is dead, you will still see quite a lot of fish, as visitors keep them well fed with park-provided nibbles. Note that snorkel gear, locker rental and the high-wire zip-line ride from the cliffs down to the water cost extra; an all-inclusive package with meals, towels and snorkel gear is an option, as are deals that include transport from Cancún. While it is theoretically possible, and often recommended by bargain hounds, to reach the reef through the adjacent *Garrafón de Castilla* beach club ($3 entrance, with its own bay for decent snorkelling), you're likely to get nabbed by vigilant park workers who can see you don't have an official life vest; you're also dodging the national park fee that goes to maintaining the reef.

▲ZIP LINE, GARRAFÓN PARK

Templo de Ixchel

Southernmost point of the island. Daily 9am–6.30pm. $3, free with entrance to Garrafón park. In the spring of 1517, Francisco Hernández de Córdoba set sail from Cuba with three ships, and first laid eyes on Mexico – specifically, this island and this unimposing Mayan temple. The temple was filled with female fertility figures, dedications to the fertility goddess Ixchel, which led the Spaniards to dub the place "the island of women". Today the temple isn't much more than a couple of low walls, but it is dramatically perched on rocky cliffs, where you can stand and imagine the conquistadors' arrival. The entrance fee also entitles you to the somewhat random modern sculpture park set up along the path out to the ruins themselves. The area

in front of the site entrance is an extension of Garrafón park, with a cluster of faux-Caribbean houses containing shops and a restaurant, as well as the old lighthouse, which provides a decent view down the length of the island.

Cuevas de los Tiburones Dormidos

5km northeast of Punta Norte. The "caves of the sleeping sharks" off the northeast coast are a major dive destination where tiger, Caribbean reef, lemon, blue and even bull sharks rest in an oxygen-rich freshwater current that lulls them into stasis. Coverage of the phenomenon by Jacques Cousteau and National Geographic in the mid-Seventies brought more visitors and thus drove some sharks away, but you'll still have a good chance of seeing the fish,

Tours to Isla Contoy

La Isleña Sea Tours, on Calle Morelos one block back from Avenida Rueda Medina, runs a relaxed faux-castaway trip to Isla Contoy, with lunch caught straight from the sea. Alternatively, you can arrange a similar jaunt through the fishermen's cooperative, at the dock at the end of Calle Madero – preferably on board Capitán Ricardo Gaitan's *Estrella del Norte* (☎998/877-1363, ☜www.isla-mujeres.net, ✉riccontoy@hotmail.com), the last wooden boat made on the island, some thirty years old. In all cases, **tours** last the whole day and include a basic breakfast, grilled fish for lunch, soft drinks and snorkel gear for about $40. For an additional $10, payable on the island, you can take a bird-watching tour with one of the resident biologists. For more information, visit ☜www.islacontoy.org.

and the rocky crags (not actual caves) are interesting to explore. As the site is in the open sea, with both unpredictable currents and sharks, only more advanced divers should make the trip, which is easily arranged through dive shops in town (see p.166).

Isla Contoy

30km north of Isla Mujeres. $3 park fee. The main day outing from Isla Mujeres, to which scores of touts devote their efforts, is a boat trip to the bird sanctu-ary of Contoy. The small island, only 8.5km long, was designated a national park in 1961, and now it's home to some 150 bird species, including large colonies of pelicans, cormorants and frigates. The calm western beaches serve as a safe nesting haven for sea turtles, while the windy eastern coast is a mix of dunes and limestone cliffs. The boat trip out is leisurely, often with stops to snorkel at reefs along the way; by lunchtime you're deposited on a small beach in a lagoon (often with several other

▼ISLA CONTOY

groups, which can dampen the isolated spirit) and given the afternoon to either relax in the sun or explore the wild setting, starting at a small welcome centre and observation tower and going along a set path into the mangroves that cover the interior of the island.

Accommodation

Belmar

Av Hidalgo 110, between C Madero and C Abasolo ☎998/877-0430, ⊛www.rolandi.com. The sunny rooms with big French doors and plenty of extras are a good deal – despite the potentially noisy location above Rolandi's pizzeria on the main nightlife drag. Doubles from $56.

Casa Maya Zazil-Há

C Zazil-Há at Playa Norte ☎998/877-0045, ⊛www.kasamaya.com.mx. This offbeat outpost of old-style Isla Mujeres, where faux Olmec heads dot the grounds and hammocks are slung between the trees, is a well-priced option directly on the beach, especially in the off-season. Free snorkel gear is available for use in the shallow protected bay out front. Rooms (with one bed) start at $70; two doubles are available for $110.

Cristalmar

On the Sac Bajo Peninsula, 500m north of Hacienda Mundaca ☎998/877-0390, ⊛www.cristalmarhotel.com. The big one- and two-bedroom suites with full kitchens and dining areas are popular with vacationing Mexican families. In addition to the beach, a pool, dive shop and game room keep everyone entertained. Not ritzy, but great staff and a solid bargain. Suites from $115.

Francis Arlene

C Guerrero 7, at C Abasolo ☎998/877-0310, ⊛www.francisarlene.com. Pretty, small, family-owned hotel with well-tended courtyards and clean (if rather exuberantly painted) rooms with frilly bedspreads and plenty of comforts, such as balconies and refrigerators. Good value, especially as there's a choice of a/c or fan. Doubles from $45.

Hotel Secreto

On the northeastern shore, adjacent to *Playa la Media Luna* ☎998/877-1039, ⊛www.hotelsecreto.com. This whitewashed modern hotel looks more Mediterranean than Mexican; amenities include enormous fluffy beds and CD players in the rooms, and a welcoming outdoor lounge, complete with overstuffed sofas, set by a pool and a partially sheltered cove. For this level of

▼HOTEL SECRETO

86

style and service, the ground-floor double rooms ($165) are a great deal; continental breakfast is included.

Mar y Sol
5km southeast from the ferry, on the bay side www.morningsinmexico .com. A hands-off apartment rental, available by the night ($40) or the week ($250). The four studios (each with two beds, a/c, a range and a fridge) are basic, but right on the beach. It's a taxi ride from the action on the north end of the island, but walking distance to a smaller village for supplies, or to Playa Lancheros for lunch.

Na Balam
C Zazil-Há at Playa Norte ☎998/877-0279, www.nabalam.com. One of the island's most comfortable hotels, with a pool, a tropical garden on the flawless beach, a good restaurant and large rooms that are elegant but not pretentious. Free yoga classes Mon–Fri. Doubles from $182.

Playa la Media Luna
On the northeastern shore ☎998/877-1124, www.playamedialuna.com. The pastel rooms each have a/c, a fridge, and a balcony overlooking the beach, which is a bit rocky, but still swimmable; there's also a pool. Nicely isolated, despite its proximity to town – walk straight up Calle Mateos to the north shore. Continental breakfast is included. Doubles from $90.

Posada Isla Mujeres
C Juárez between C Abasolo and C Madero (no tel). This small budget hotel has sparkling white rooms with fans and very new fixtures. If no one's there to greet you, inquire at *Posada Suemi* around the corner at Calle Matam-

oros between Calle Juárez and Avenida Medina. Rooms from $20.

Roca Mar
C Bravo at C Guerrero, behind the church next to the *zócalo* ☎998/877-0101. One of the island's oldest hotels, *Roca Mar* is very well maintained. The big rooms all have balconies, and the small restaurant overlooks the Caribbean. The beach is rocky, but there is a decent-size pool. Rates start at $45.

Suites Los Arcos
Av Hidalgo 58, between C Matamoros and C Abasolo ☎998/877-1343, www.suiteslosarcos.com. Clean, modern rooms with kitchenettes and a/c; the quieter ones in the back have bigger balconies too. Doubles from $70; discounts for week-long stays.

Villa Las Brisas
2.5km south from the ferry, on the Caribbean side ☎998/888-0342, www.villalasbrisas.com. A beautifully designed guesthouse perched above dramatic crashing surf (swim in the pretty pool instead). The five rooms (from $135), all have king-size beds and fantastic feather pillows; delicious full breakfast is included.

Shops

Artesanías Glenssy
C Mateos between C Hidalgo and C Guerrero, across from the post office. Tucked in a small shed next to a *torta* stand is this workshop producing exceptionally beautiful papier-mâché masks and headdresses painted in elaborate colours and patterns. The hours are erratic, and the artist isn't really geared to selling to tour-

ists, but it's worth taking a peek at the excellent craftwork when the shop is open.

Cafés

Café Cito

C Juárez at C Matamoros. Visit this colourful, cheery breakfast and lunch spot for healthy yoghurt-granola plates or more decadent crepes and waffles, along with very good coffee.

Cazuela M&J

At the Roca Mar hotel, C Bravo at the ocean. Daily 7am–2pm. Enjoy a fine ocean view at this casual café serving big, mostly Mexican breakfasts for about $6. The signature egg dish is a sort of omelette baked in a *cazuela*, or earthenware casserole. Big glasses of *chaya* juice are another healthy option.

Cocktelería Picus

Av Rueda Medina just north of ferry landings. This small beachfront hut serves fresh and inexpensive ceviches and shrimp cocktails ($4–9). Lunch only in the low season.

Restaurants

Le Bistro Français

C Matamoros 29, at Av Hidalgo. Daily 8am–noon, 6–10pm. French-influenced restaurant with a varied, inventive and delicious menu at reasonable prices – from about $7 for fish with fennel and capers to $24 for lobster tail. Good breakfasts too.

Casa Rolandi

At the *Villa Rolandi* hotel, at the end of the Sac Bajo peninsula ☎998/877-0500, ⊛www.rolandi.com. The menu at this northern Italian restaurant – the best dishes come from the wood-burning oven – is the same as at its Cancún counterpart, but the setting here is superior, on a covered terrace overlooking the turquoise bay; at night, lights on the mainland glimmer in the distance.

Jax Bar & Grill

Av Medina at C Mateos, next to the lighthouse ☎998/877-1218. Daily 11am till late. The place to go for a dose of Americana: giant hamburgers are the house speciality, and kids will enjoy plenty

PLACES Isla Mujeres

▼ARTESANÍAS GLENSSY

▲MENU, LE BISTRO FRANÇAIS

Isla Mujeres PLACES

of other dishes tailored to their tastes. The upstairs lounge has a mellower atmosphere than the ground-floor bar, and the beers are very well chilled.

La Lomita

C Juárez 25-B, two blocks south of the plaza. Lunch only. Locals line up for a helping of the chef-owner's daily specials, anything from bean soup and *chiles rellenos* to pan-fried fish with salsa verde. Fantastic home cooking, worth the hike up the small hill.

Lonchería Alexía y Geovanny

C Guerrero between C Mateos and C Matamoros. One of several bargain lunch stalls clustered here, proudly serving up good, fresh ceviche ($4) or set-price dishes like spicy pork chops served with rice, beans and tortillas (also $4).

Rolandi's

Av Hidalgo between C Madero and C Abasolo. Part of a small family-run chain serving great wood-oven pizza, lobster, fresh fish and other northern Italian dishes with salads. Prices start around $6 for pizzas.

El Sombrero d'Gomar

Av Hidalgo at C Madero. Hearty portions at reasonable prices are the draw at this two-storey palapa restaurant on the main avenue. Stick with Mexican staples like enchiladas; the *chilaquiles* (tortillas smothered in spicy tomato sauce) are a good breakfast option.

Velazquez

Av Medina at C Matamoros. Conveniently located right next to the dock for the fishermen's cooperative, this bare-bones restaurant's speciality is the catch of the day – get it grilled, fried or *en mojo de ajo* (with long-simmered garlic) for between $6 and $10.

Zazil Ha

At the *Na Balam* hotel, C Zazil–Há. Modern Mayan and Caribbean flavours, in the form of tropical-fruit salsas and a variety of seafood dishes, are on the menu at this torch-lit beachfront restaurant. Vegetarians will also appreciate the good selection of meatless dishes. Entrées are a little steep (between $10 and $15) – but you're also paying for fancy presentation and the gorgeous setting.

Bars

Bally-Hoo

Av Medina near C Abasolo. Swap tales with yachties at this casual, wood-panelled bar under a palapa. Strategically placed on the marina pier, it's the designated hangout for anyone looking to crew a boat.

Buho's

Playa Norte at C Carlos Lazo, in front of *Cabañas María del Mar*. In high season, this beach bar tends to be the liveliest and most popular, with loud rock music, swinging hammock chairs and a well-attended happy hour in the late afternoon.

Hemingway

C Guerrero at C Matamoros. A locals' cantina in a Caribbean-style wood house with a porch – the clientele is almost entirely men, and can get rowdy on weekends.

Om

C Matamoros between C Juárez and C Hidalgo. A groovy international-flavoured lounge with pillows on the floor, twenty types of herbal tea and personal beer taps at each table. No particular Mexican flair, but a fine place to meet other travellers.

La Peña

C Guerrero on the main plaza ☎998/845-7384. Daily 7.30pm–3am. An upstairs bar-lounge with a view of the Caribbean, drawing a younger crowd with fresh-ground coffee, cocktails, DJs and a big movie screen.

Clubs

Nitrox Club VIP

C Matamoros between C Guerrero and C Hidalgo ☎998/887-0568. Wed–Sun 9pm–3am. The only disco in town, *Nitrox* is frequented by locals and tourists alike. Wed is ladies night; Fri has Latin music, with free dance classes from 10pm till midnight. Cover is rarely more than $2.

▼BUHO'S BEACH BAR

Puerto Morelos

In sharp contrast with fast-paced neighbour Cancún, just twenty minutes away, **Puerto Morelos** is a mellow fishing village where the afternoon siesta is still observed by most businesses. The biggest attraction is the northern edge of the thriving Mesoamerican Barrier Reef, less than a kilometre offshore and barely touched by tourists. In town, you'll find no sights save for the local icon, an old lighthouse knocked Tower of Pisa-style by a hurricane. For such a small population, Puerto Morelos does, however, offer a remarkably large number of excellent restaurants, ranging from genre-defining tacos to modern-fusion panache. A little way inland, a cluster of beautiful cenotes is just beginning to draw visitors; south of town, the coast is occupied primarily by resorts, but a few quiet spots still harbour rustic hotels and simple restaurants serving the classic beach meal of ceviche and grilled fish along with ice-cold beers.

PUERTO MORELOS COAST

ACCOMMODATION

Acamaya Reef	A
Bahía Xcalacoco	H
Ceiba del Mar	C
Coco's Cabañas	G
Maroma	E
Maya Echo B&B	B
La Posada de Capitán Lafitte	F
Rancho Libertad	D

Parque Nacional Arrecifes de Puerto Morelos

300m offshore from the town centre. $2. Designated a national marine park in 2000, the reef in front of Puerto Morelos is the northernmost end of the enormous Mesoamerican Barrier Reef, which stretches all the way to Honduras. The area is easily accessible by boat and relatively uncrowded with visitors – which makes it a particularly convenient place to learn to dive. Because of its park status, the reef can be visited only with a guide (see pp.165–6), who can point out loggerhead turtles, spotted eagle rays and giant lobsters. The shallow coral gardens here – ideal for snorkellers – are not as vast as those on Cozumel, but harbour a huge variety of life and teem with iridescent fish; divers will want to tour the deeper coral canyons. Advanced divers can visit a couple of wreck sites, including a sunken naval destroyer that lies about 4km offshore.

Ruta de los Cenotes

West from Hwy-307 1km south of the Puerto Morelos junction.

A concrete neo-Maya arch marks the start of this dirt road leading inland – a government effort to draw visitors to this patch of dense forest punctuated by cenotes, all of which charge about $5 admission. So far the tourist interest has been slight, so you'll likely have the swimming holes to yourself. Sixteen kilometres along the route you pass the very small village of Central Vallarta, a former camp for *chicleros* harvesting sap for the chewing-gum industry. The first cenote, which requires a bit of bushwhacking to reach, is Siete Bocas, an extended network of underground caverns; to get there, follow the signs at Central Vallarta and hike 10 minutes off the road. The next cenote is Boca del Puma, about 1km past the village on the right side of the road, where the owner has installed a long zip-line ride and an observation tower; mountain bikes are also available for rent. Verde Lucero, another 2km along on the left, is named for its emerald-green water; there's a smaller zip-line here for swinging into the pool. Finally, a surfboard sign further along

▲ PUERTO MORELOS' LIGHTHOUSE

PLACES Puerto Morelos

on the right signals Tres Bocas, a string of several small cenotes linked by the barest of paths through the forest. A few rustic cabins here rent for $60 per night (for up to four people).

Although the road is passable in a rental car (or you can hire a taxi at the Puerto Morelos junction for $40 for two hours), you'll get more out of your visit with a small tour and a guide who's familiar with the local plants and animals (see pp.165–6).

Visiting Puerto Morelos

Buses from the Cancún airport (9 daily, 10.30am–9.30pm; $3.50) and the Cancún bus station (every 10min; $1.60) stop on Hwy-307 near Puerto Morelos, where you can hire a taxi for the 2km ride into town ($2). Buses ($1.60) also head north from Playa del Carmen to Puerto Morelos every ten minutes.

An official **information kiosk** is located at the highway intersection (daily 9am–4pm).

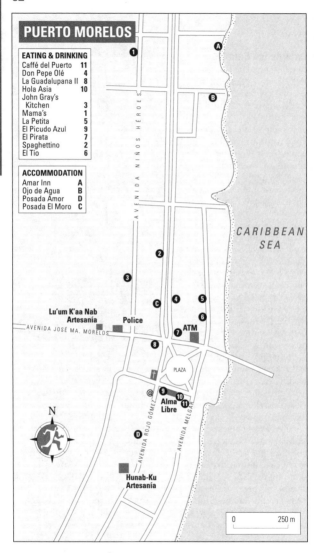

PUERTO MORELOS

EATING & DRINKING

Caffé del Puerto	11
Don Pepe Olé	4
La Guadalupana II	8
Hola Asia	10
John Gray's Kitchen	3
Mama's	1
La Petita	5
El Picudo Azul	9
El Pirata	7
Spaghettino	2
El Tío	6

ACCOMMODATION

Amar Inn	A
Ojo de Agua	B
Posada Amor	D
Posada El Moro	C

AVENIDA NIÑOS HÉROES

CARIBBEAN SEA

Lu'um K'aa Nab Artesanía

Police

AVENIDA JOSÉ MA. MORELOS

ATM

PLAZA

@

Alma Libre

AVENIDA ROJO GÓMEZ

AVENIDA MELGAR

N

Hunab-Ku Artesanía

0   250 m

Jardín Botánico Dr Alfredo Barrera Marín

East side of Hwy-307, 1km south of the Puerto Morelos junction (also signposted as Yaax Ché). Mon–Sat 9am–5pm. $7. The 148-acre botanical gardens are a worth-while introduction to the native flora of the coastal state of Quintana Roo. A three-kilometre path leads through medicinal plants, ferns, palms, some tumbledown Maya ruins and a mock-up *chiclero* camp,

▲JARDIN BOTÁNICO

where you can see how the sap of the *zapote* (sapodilla) tree is tapped before being used in the production of chewing gum. A vast untended chunk of forest is inhabited by spider monkeys (though they usually keep out of sight); a trail leads to a viewing platform above the canopy. If you're particularly interested in botany, it's worth hiring a guide, either at the site or through one of the several tour operators in Puerto Morelos that run day-trips (see pp.161–2).

Playa Acamaya

5km north of Puerto Morelos, near the *Acamaya Reef* campground. Steady breezes and minimal water traffic have made this beach very popular with fans of the nascent sport of kiteboarding. Ikarus, the major school in the area, gives most of its classes here, and can provide you with a no-frills board if you haven't brought your own gear – or you can arrange lessons and rent equipment from their shop in Playa del Carmen (see p.166). And, even for spectators, the fast, elegant moves of the experts are a fine diversion.

Paseo de Manglares

2km north of Puerto Morelos, across the street from *Ceiba del Mar.* Free. Some three hundred bird species – such as roseate spoonbills, herons and many migratory songbirds – reside in the mangrove swamps that line the Caribbean coast. The trees, which thrive in brackish water, are an intrinsic part of sea life, too, as the mineral-rich run-off from their roots flows out to sea and nourishes the coral reefs. A raised boardwalk, built and maintained by the *Ceiba del Mar* hotel, runs for about a kilometre through a large group of tangled trees. Although mangrove clusters can be found in many places along the water in the Yucatán, this is a unique opportunity to explore this complex ecosystem on your own, as the swamps – also home to crocodiles – aren't safe to wade through without a guide. Go early in the morning or in the late afternoon to catch the most bird activity.

Punta Brava

2km south of Puerto Morelos. Follow signs for "Marina El Cid" to find this quiet patch of undevel-

▲ PUNTA BRAVA BEACH

oped beach just south of town. Although there are no services (except for a café in the marina just to the north), the beach is generally kept clean and is empty on weekdays, with very clear, shallow water. On weekends, it's a popular day-outing for Cancún residents.

Playa Xcalacoco

10km south of Puerto Morelos. Follow signs for "Punta Bete" east from Hwy-307, at the Cristal depository, then take the right fork on the dirt road. Thick with palms thanks to its former use as a coconut plantation, Playa Xcalacoco is a quiet, ungroomed spot for playing at castaway. A basic restaurant, *Juanito's*, serves up cold beers and ceviche; otherwise, there's not much to do but lie in the sun (chairs rent for $7 per day) or under the shade of a palm tree. It's also possible to camp here ($4.50 per person) or check in to a couple of hotels just to the north and south, should you find yourself not wanting to leave.

Accommodation

Acamaya Reef

5km north of Puerto Morelos on the coast road ☎987/871-0132, ⊛www .acamayareef.com. A pleasantly ramshackle beachfront RV park (from $15) and camping spot ($9 per person) just north of Puerto Morelos – look for a signposted turn-off from Hwy-307 near the entrance to the Crococun zoo. The owner, a French artist, cooks tasty meals, and his work dots the grounds. Cabañas with private bath are also available, from $47.

Amar Inn

500m north of the main plaza on the seafront ☎998/871-0026, ⊜amar_inn@hotmail.com. Though not far from the centre of town, this bohemian, family-run hotel feels more like a remote beachfront artist's colony. The eight large rooms and cabañas are breezy and individually decorated – some have high ceilings, loft beds and kitchenettes. A delicious Mexican breakfast is included. Doubles from $35.

Bahía Xcalacoco

At the end of the right fork off the Punta Bete road ☎984/804-5848. Rooms are very nicely maintained and attractive at this remote-feeling beach hotel with minimal electricity about 500m south of Playa Xcalacoco. The helpful owners can arrange snorkelling and fishing trips and fetch groceries from town for long-stay guests. Camping is also an option ($4 per person). Doubles from $35.

Ceiba del Mar

2km north of Puerto Morelos on the coast road ☎998/872-8060, ⊛www .ceibadelmar.com. The 125 rooms at this spa resort are decorated

▲AMAR INN

in earth tones and natural fibres, with ocean views from the balconies or the big bathtubs. A vast freeform pool makes up for a somewhat shallow beach. In the pantheon of small luxury hotels along this coast, *Ceiba del Mar* is not as well appointed as *Maroma* (below), but it's not so isolated, and it has a full sauna with wet and dry rooms and a cold plunge. Continental breakfast is included; a half-board package is an option. Doubles from $355.

Coco's Cabañas

At the end of the left fork off the Punta Bete road ☎998/874-7056, ✉marsilhel@hotmail.com. This charming Swiss-owned hide-away has just five cosy, colourfully furnished round cabañas, a small pool surrounded by wild greenery, and a restaurant serving very good European cuisine. Though not directly on the beach, there's easy access to the water. Rates start at $45 for a single queen-size bed.

Maroma

8km south of Puerto Morelos, east of Hwy-307 ☎998/872-8200, ⊕www .orient-expresshotels.com. Elegant yet informal, with a strong Mexican style, this is the best of the coast's luxury hotels – in part because it started as a small private home and has grown almost organically over three decades. Spa treatments include a refreshing and therapeutic *temazcal* (sweat lodge), while the restaurant's Spanish chef prepares imaginative, fresh cuisine such as ceviche layered with tomato-broth gelatine "noodles". Full breakfast, airport transfer and one snorkel trip are included in the rates, which start at $410.

Maya Echo B&B

3km north of Puerto Morelos on the coast road ☎998/871-0136, ⊕www .mayaecho.com. A longtime Puerto Morelos resident

▼CEIBA DEL MAR HOTEL

dedicated to sustainable tourism manages this comfortable guesthouse with a friendly, casual feel. Each of the three rooms has two twin beds; one has a/c. Downstairs opens onto a patio and garden. Rates (from $50) include a lavish full breakfast.

Ojo de Agua
400m north of the plaza on the seafront ☎987/871-0027, ⊛www .ojo-de-agua.com. Popular with divers, this hotel has 36 bright, clean rooms with modern decor; some have a/c, while others have kitchenettes. The pool is giant, and the clean beach out front is dotted with palm trees. Live bands occasionally play at the palapa-roof restaurant on the sand. One perk: rooms with ocean views don't cost more. Doubles from $56.

Posada Amor
Av Rojo Gómez in the second block south of the plaza ☎998/871-0033, ⓔpos_amor@hotmail.com. A reputation for friendly service has made *Amor* one of the longest-running hotels in town, despite not being right on the beach. The quirky rooms – clearly built in phases and all individually decorated – vary significantly: a few are the least expensive around, with shared bath; some others are more comfortably furnished and worth the extra money. Doubles from $20.

La Posada del Capitán Lafitte
9km south of Puerto Morelos, east of Hwy-307 ☎984/873-0212, ⊛www .capitanlafitte.com. This hassle-free beach resort chucks all the scheduled-activity hoopla and replaces it with funky touches like seaside beer delivery by burro. Repeat guests, some of whom have been coming since

the hotel opened more than thirty years ago, book a good portion of the rooms; children are also very welcome. Rates include breakfast and dinner. Doubles from $200.

Posada El Moro
Av Rojo Gómez 17, just north of the plaza ☎987/871-0159, ⊛www .posadaelmoro.com. Ten clean rooms, some with kitchens, in a pretty little garden. Amenities, including a small pool, laundry facilities and a travel agency, are excellent for the price, with doubles from $45.

Sak Ol
1km south of the plaza on the seafront ☎998/871-0181, ⊛www.ranchosakol .com. A stay at these casual two-storey thatched cabañas with hanging beds includes a large breakfast buffet with fruit and cereal; guests can also use the communal kitchen. Enjoy a massage ($45 per hour) either on the wide beach or in the shady gardens. Doubles start at $69.

Shops

Alma Libre
South side of the plaza ☎998/871-0713, ⊛www.almalibrebooks.com. Oct–May Tues–Sat 10am–3pm & 6–9pm; Sun 4–9pm. With some twenty thousand volumes to choose from, this is probably Mexico's most extensive second-hand English-language bookshop. There's also a solid selection of new books about the area's natural and archeological attractions. If you're in town for a while, sign up for the email newsletter on town events. The helpful owners also transfer digital camera images to a CD for a small fee.

▲ HUNAB-KU ARTESANÍA

Cafés

La Guadalupana II
West side of the plaza at the main access road. Hot, delicious and inexpensive tacos are cooked up nightly at this small, popular stand on the main square.

Mama's
Av Niños Heroés three blocks north of the plaza. Closed Mon. Homey American-owned breakfast and lunch joint offering breakfast burritos with veggie chorizo ($5), oatmeal, fruit smoothies and a whole range of baked goods.

El Picudo Azul
South side of the plaza ☎998/871-0115. Closed Wed. Choose from tacos in all forms, from shrimp to *arrachera* (grilled skirt steak). It's pricier than *La Guadalupana II*, but it has a pleasant café atmosphere and is open all day.

El Tío
Av Melgar just north of the plaza. A hole in the wall serving fish tacos at breakfast and very cheap *tortas* (Mexican-style sandwiches) and other standard Yucatecan snacks for lunch.

Hunab-Ku Artesanía
Av Rojo Gómez two blocks south of the plaza. Locals call this the "Mayan mini-mall", but the shops are far from tacky, with very good-quality handicrafts such as hammocks and embroidered clothing, much of which is eventually sold in Cancún for twice the price.

Lu'um K'aa Nab Artesanía
On the main access road at Av Rojo Gómez. This small palapa kiosk is where women from nearby Central Vallarta sell their very reasonably priced embroidery work, such as clothing, aprons, dolls and hats. The work is part of a women's development program (🖥 www.mayanwomensproject.com), and profits from the attractive items are returned directly to their community.

Restaurants

Caffé del Puerto
Av Melgar just south of the plaza ☎998/871-0735. For lunch, stop in at this casual spot for inexpensive salads and sandwiches (around $4). The even better deal is the $10 set menu at dinner, with the selection changing daily and reflecting the owners' eclectic tastes, from Mexican to Thai – go early, as they can run out.

Hola Asia

South side of the plaza. Get your fix of General Tso's chicken ($6) at this nouveau noodle house, or sample other Asian delicacies such as Thai fish with tamarind ($9) or Indonesian-style coconut shrimp ($11). The rooftop tiki bar is breezy and scenic at sunset – and the main expat hangout in town.

John Gray's Kitchen

Av Niños Héroes north of the plaza ☎998/871-0665. Closed Sun. Guests often make the short drive down from Cancún for dinner at this small, casually elegant restaurant. The owner is an ex-*Ritz-Carlton* chef, and his gourmet background shows: the daily menu features simple, smart combos like pan-roasted duck breast with *chipotle*, tequila and honey. With most entrées under $20 and generous portions, it's quite a bargain too.

La Petita

Av Melgar half a block north of the plaza. Mon–Sat 10am–6pm. This small wooden house is a fishermen's hangout and a local favourite for enjoying the fresh catch of the day, sold by the kilo and available fried or grilled, or in a ceviche. A whole *pescado frito* and a few beers will set you back about $10.

El Pirata

North side of the plaza. Hamburgers and Mexican staples like big, saucy enchiladas and decent tacos make up the menu at this small open-air restaurant with economical prices ($3–7 for sandwiches and full meals). A great informal hangout spot, with chatty owners and all manner of people stopping through.

Spaghettino

Av Rojo Gómez a block and a half north of the plaza ☎998/871-0573. An informal Italian restaurant with a Euro café feel, offering pizza (starting at $6) and panini ($4) or bigger meals of handmade pastas (from $7).

Bars

Don Pepe Olé

Av Rojo Gómez north of the plaza. A sometimes rowdy local bar scene, complete with buckets of beer on ice, starting in the afternoon; karaoke is the entertainment of choice once the sun goes down. The evening is also the time for a Mexican dinner menu, which is quite good. If you're craving more English-language entertainment, hit the American-owned *Cantina Habañero* across the street.

▼LA PETITA RESTAURANT

Playa del Carmen

Once a sleepy fishing village, Playa del Carmen (or simply Playa) has mushroomed in recent years into a high-style party town for Europeans and Mexico City jet-setters. It still holds its own as an attractive destination, with nightlife that's more casual and less frenetic than Cancún's, sophisticated cuisine, hotels for all budgets and a wide range of shops. Playa Norte, the beach on the north end of town that's dominated by a hip beach club, is one of the prettiest on the coast, with dazzling white sand and gloriously clear sea, and the offshore reef is almost as spectacular here as in Cozumel. Though booming Playa sprawls west, the central tourist district is compact and easily covered on foot or bicycle.

Avenida 5

Between C 1 Sur and C 28. Playa's main tourist thoroughfare, commonly called La Quinta, was once a dirt track dotted with a few cabañas. Today Avenida 5 is a pedestrian route lined with cocktail lounges, souvenir shops, small hotels and stylish restaurants – an errant *TGI Friday*'s is the exception to what is otherwise a relatively attractively developed, franchise-free zone. In high season, the stretch from Avenida Juárez to Avenida Constituyentes is packed with day-trippers from Cozumel, cruise-ship passengers and assorted bikini-clad tourists and sun-bronzed residents. Nightfall sees cruising of a different kind, with revellers geared up to drink and dance. North of Constituyentes is the quieter, still developing section called Playa Norte, or North Beach, for the gorgeous sand that fronts it. It's also known as Little Italy – head up this way for a dinner of pasta handmade by a Sicilian expat.

Playa Caribe

Seafront between Av Juárez and C 16. In recent years, Playa's central beach, fronting calm, pale green water and dotted with boats,

Visiting Playa del Carmen

Buses depart every ten minutes from Cancún's central bus station to Playa del Carmen ($3.50; 1hr), or you can take a bus directly from the Cancún airport (9 daily; 1hr) for $6.50. Both of these buses arrive at the central bus station on Avenida Juárez at Avenida 5 (another station for long-haul buses is located at Avenida 20 between calles 12 and 14).

From Cozumel, **ferries** make the half-hour trip from the pier in downtown San Miguel almost hourly between 5am and 11pm; the last boat from Playa returns at midnight ($9 one way, or $12.50 for a same-day return). You will arrive either at Calle 1 Sur (Mexico Waterjets boats) or Avenida Consituyentes (Ultramar service).

The town's well-stocked **tourist office** is located on Avenida Juárez at Avenida 15 (daily 9am–9pm ☎984/873-2804, ✉turismo@solidaridad.gob.mx).

PLACES

Playa del Carmen

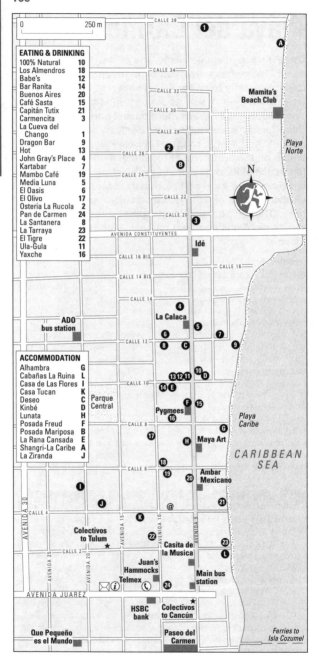

0 ————— 250 m

EATING & DRINKING

100% Natural	10
Los Almendros	18
Babe's	12
Bar Ranita	14
Buenos Aires	20
Café Sasta	15
Capitán Tutix	21
Carmencita	3
La Cueva del Chango	1
Dragon Bar	9
Hot	13
John Gray's Place	4
Kartabar	7
Mambo Café	19
Media Luna	5
El Oasis	6
El Olivo	17
Osteria La Rucola	2
Pan de Carmen	24
La Santanera	8
La Tarraya	23
El Tigre	22
Ula-Gula	11
Yaxche	16

ACCOMMODATION

Alhambra	G
Cabañas La Ruina	L
Casa de Las Flores	I
Casa Tucan	K
Deseo	C
Kinbé	D
Lunata	H
Posada Freud	F
Posada Mariposa	B
La Rana Cansada	E
Shangri-La Caribe	A
La Ziranda	J

CALLE 38
CALLE 34
CALLE 32
CALLE 30
CALLE 28
CALLE 26
CALLE 24
CALLE 22
CALLE 20
AVENIDA CONSTITUYENTES
CALLE 16 BIS
CALLE 16
CALLE 14 BIS
CALLE 14
CALLE 12
CALLE 10
CALLE 8
CALLE 6
CALLE 4
CALLE 2
AVENIDA JUAREZ

AVENIDA 30
AVENIDA 25
AVENIDA 20
AVENIDA 15
AVENIDA 10
AVENIDA 5

Mamita's Beach Club

Playa Norte

N

Idé

La Calaca

ADO bus station

Parque Central

Pygmees

Maya Art

Playa Caribe

CARIBBEAN SEA

Ambar Mexicano

Colectivos to Tulum

Juan's Hammocks
Telmex

Casita de la Musica

Main bus station

HSBC bank

Colectivos to Cancún

Que Pequeño es el Mundo

Paseo del Carmen

Ferries to Isla Cozumel

has become noticeably eroded, particularly between calles 6 and 14, with a narrowing sandy frontage and rocks popping up in the water. A reclamation project is underway, but the sand shifts from week to week, so it's impossible to track the best place for laying out. As the sand is a bit thin, it's worth shelling out a few dollars for a chair rental at one of the hotels or beach clubs (some of which also offer parasailing, snorkelling or catamaran trips). Or simply enjoy a drink at one of the numerous bars and restaurants and take in the lively social scene, which kicks off with happy hour around 5pm.

Mamita's Beach Club

Seafront at C 28. A short trek north of the central tourist throng, this club at Playa Norte sports deeper sand than Playa Caribe and plenty of room to spread out, with chairs and umbrellas for rent as well as changing rooms, a pool, a play-ground for kids and a very good (if slightly expensive) restaurant. The dive shop here, Sealife, runs snorkel tours ($20, 1.5hr). The northern half of the club's beach has a hipper feel, with a separate small bar with a DJ, hanging beds and a volleyball court. The

bar is often open in the early evening after the rest of the club has closed, and occasionally hosts evening dance parties too.

Punta Zubul

800m north of *Mamita's Beach Club.* Once an isolated, windswept patch of sand, this point just north of town has long lured people with its easy access to the colourful reef offshore. A generic resort now looms nearby, but the vibrant coral outcroppings are still there, as is the *Zubul Reef Club* palapa-roof bar, which rents snorkel gear to those who make the trek up the beach. The reef lies about 200m out, past a clutch of fishing boats – a long swim but an easy trip in a rented kayak ($10 per hour), or as part of a group on a catamaran with the local guide who sets up shop here (about $20 per person).

Parque Central

Av 15 between C 8 and C 10. This block-square park in front of Playa's town hall is a nicely groomed patch of lawn with a small amphitheatre that occasionally hosts theatre and musical performances (check with the tourist office or ⓦwww.playamayanews.com for listings). To one side of the park

▼PARQUE CENTRAL

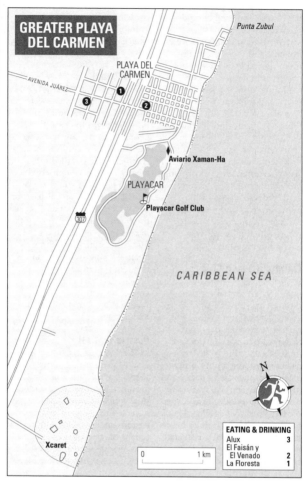

GREATER PLAYA DEL CARMEN

Punta Zubul

PLAYA DEL CARMEN

AVENIDA JUÁREZ

1

3

2

Aviario Xaman-Ha

PLAYACAR

Playacar Golf Club

307

CARIBBEAN SEA

N

Xcaret

0   1 km

EATING & DRINKING

Alux	3
El Faisán y	
El Venado	2
La Floresta	1

are six stelae inscribed with the verses of the "Himno de Quintana Roo". This ode captures the fledgling state's pioneer spirit, its role as a refuge for the indigenous Maya and its place in history as the site of the first *mestizaje*, the intermixing of Spanish and Indian races that literally gave birth to modern Mexico – a strong point of pride in the Yucatán. By evening, the park is a tranquil local hang-out,

as kids take to the ramps on skateboards, while older women chat on the benches.

Playacar

South of C 1 Sur. This 880-acre development of resorts, condos and private homes just south of town is an inviting locale for a shady stroll or bike ride. Beaches here, if they're not fronting a big resort, are often deserted. Winding Avenida Xaman-Ha is the main artery, with cul-de-sacs leading to beach properties, tennis courts and remnants of more than fifteen Mayan structures (the major ruins are marked with signs off the main road; don't expect any explanatory signage). On the inland side is the vast Playacar Golf Club. If you're staying here, be aware that the walk up to town takes between ten and thirty minutes.

Aviario Xaman-Ha

Paseo Xaman-Ha, Playacar. Daily 9am–5pm. $15. Admission is somewhat steep, but this aviary provides a great opportunity to view local wildlife if you're short of time. You can see some sixty species of native birds, including pink flamingos and delicately fringed great egrets, along with iguanas, turtles and not-so-exotic squirrels. Dedicated birders should bring their own binoculars; photographers may use tripods.

Xcaret

Hwy-307 6km south of Playa del Carmen @ www.xcaretcancun.com. Mon–Sat 8.30am–9.45pm, Sun 8.30am–6pm. $49, kids $25. The most highly touted tourist attraction along the Caribbean coast, Xcaret is a huge, somewhat bizarre eco-archeological theme park that retains a relatively wild feel despite the throngs of visitors. Travellers on longer stays will be able to find all Xcaret's attractions elsewhere, minus the crowds, but for anyone with a limited amount of time, and especially anyone with children, the park gives visitors a chance to experience all of the natural features of the Yucatán, plus Maya-style ballgames and pony rides.

The grounds of Xcaret include an extensive system of cenotes and caverns, some of which were artificially widened to create more than a kilometre of subterranean rivers down which you can swim, snorkel or simply float with the help of neon innertubes. The rivers empty into a large lagoon, where there's a sandy beach, a protected area for novice snorkellers and the obligatory dolphin-swim pens. Additional natural attractions include a botanical garden, an enormous butterfly habitat, a cave full of native bats, an aquarium and a

▼XCARET

sea turtle reserve, while fiddler crabs and howler monkeys roam wild throughout the grounds.

Alongside is a "Maya village" complete with artisans working on traditional crafts, as well as some small authentic ruins. At night, a giant arena hosts an extravaganza of music, dance and "ancient ritual"; if it trades heavily on the mystique of the Maya, at least the production value is very high. And when the crowds get too thick, an open-air chapel on the park's highest hill provides quiet calm and a fine view.

Bus-and-entrance packages are available through every big hotel in Cancún and Playa del Carmen. Mayab buses stop near Xcaret on Hwy-307, or it's an easy drive from Cancún (1hr) or Playa (5min).

▼CASA DE LAS FLORES

Accommodation

Alhambra

On the beach at C 8 ☎984/873-0735, ⓦwww.alhambra-hotel.net. With gleaming white a/c rooms and a small pool, this is the strongest, best-value beachfront option. The exotic Moorish-look structure is a bit out of place, but is a fitting locale for the daily yoga classes and deep treatments offered by the resident massage therapist. Doubles, including full breakfast, start at $99.

Cabañas La Ruina

C 2 between Av 5 and the beach ☎ & ℻984/873-0405. Playa's most sociable and economical place to stay, on the beach with its own Maya ruin on the grounds. Options include camping space ($5 per person), a few hammock hooks and concrete bungalows with or without private bath (from $20).

Casa de Las Flores

Av 20 no. 150, between C 4 and C 6 ☎984/873-2898, ⓦwww .hotelcasadelasflores.com. Worth the four-block walk to the beach, this hacienda-style hotel features well-tended grounds, a small pool and clean rooms decorated with colourful bedspreads and carved wood – all at a very good price for this level of design. A few singles (fan only) are a deal at $40, while doubles with a/c start at $60.

Casa Tucan

C 4 between Av 10 and Av 15 ☎984/873-0283, ⓦwww.casatucan.de. A Playa institution and still one of the best bargains, the rambling *Casa Tucan* has spotless rooms, some of which have palapa roofs and shared bath, and excellent-value studios. A big swimming

▲ LUNATA

pool, a friendly restaurant and a generally mellow vibe all contribute to its longstanding popularity. Doubles from $22.

Deseo

Av 5 at C 12 ☎984/879-3620, ⊛www .hoteldeseo.com. This ultra-trendy boutique hotel is stocked with loads of clever details such as relaxing electronica piped into the minimalist rooms. An equally chic clientele lounges at the poolside bar, *Fly*. Rooms, all with one bed only, start at $148, with a tasty continental breakfast included. (Also look for the brand-new *Básico* hotel, down the street at Calle 10: equally sharp design, for slightly lower rates.)

Kinbé

C 10 between Av 1 and Av 5 ☎984/873-0441, ⊛ www.kinbe.com. Small, friendly Italian-run hotel with a roof deck and comfortable rooms (all with a/c) featuring bright bedspreads and contemporary Cuban paintings; a couple of rooms have a great view of the water. Guests get discounts at *Mamita's Beach Club* in Playa Norte – or you can walk straight to the sea, one block away. Standard rooms ($50) have one double bed; two-bed rooms start at $60.

Lunata

Av 5 between C 6 and C 8 ☎984/873-0884, ⊛www.lunata.com. This attractive town house is done up like a hacienda: the ceilings in the ten spacious rooms are finished with heavy wood beams, and the large bathrooms are trimmed in Mexican tile. With a location on Avenida 5, the rooms at the front can be noisy. Continental breakfast (included in the rate) is served in a walled garden. Standard rooms ($99) have one queen bed; only suites ($139) have two double beds.

Posada Freud

Av 5 between C 8 and C 10 ☎984/873-0601, ⊛www.posadafreud .com. Pretty rooms with colourful hand-painted furniture smack in the middle of the action at reasonable (and often negotiable) rates. Ground-floor basic rooms ($47) can be a little loud – it's worth springing for a back, upstairs room (from $60, with a/c and fridge), or, if you have a big group, the three-bedroom penthouse ($700 for four nights).

Posada Mariposa

Av 5 between C 24 and C 26 ☎984/873-3886, ⊛www.posada -mariposa.com. Quiet hotel overgrown with tropical plants in the

Little Italy area. Rooms (from $55) have optional a/c and are painted with whimsical ocean-theme murals; six apartments with balconies and full kitchens are also an option (from $75).

La Rana Cansada

C 10 no. 132, between Av 5 and Av 10 ☎984/873-0389, ⊛www.ranacansada .com. One of the oldest hotels in Playa, *La Rana Cansada* is friendly, sparkling clean and laid-back with a big lounge, kitchen facilities and a range of room options, including a smart two-level suite with beer delivery from the bar downstairs. Doubles from $50.

Shangri-La Caribe

C 38 on the beach ☎ 1-800/538 -6802 for US reservations, ⊛www .mexicoholiday.com. A small-scale resort, located north of the fray of Playa proper but an easy walk down the beach to the action. The grounds are very well laid out, and with two restaurants and pools, the place never feels crowded. The sand here is fine and deep, and an on-site dive shop runs trips. Rates, including breakfast and dinner, start at $195.

La Ziranda

C 4 between C 15 and C 20 ☎& ☎984/873-3929, ⊛www .hotellaziranda.com. At this serene little hotel, the spacious, simple rooms (some with a/c) are done up in soothing monochromes; each has a balcony overlooking lush greenery or a big, well-groomed backyard. A solid bargain and seldom full. Doubles from $35.

Shopping

Ambar Mexicano

Av 5 between C 4 and C 6. This small store displays glowing chunks of amber in distinctive silver settings, from relatively low prices ($20 for a simple pendant) to stratospheric ones for the largest pieces with insects preserved inside. The sales environment is blessedly low-pressure compared to many of the big jewellery stores on the strip. There's another storefront on Avenida 5 between calles 10 and 12.

La Calaca

Av 5 between C 12 and C 14. Traditional wood masks are the speciality at this well-stocked

▼SHANGRI-LA CARIBE

▲ CASITA DE LA MUSICA

folk-art shop, along with many smaller souvenir items, such as little skeleton dioramas, punched tin lanterns and elaborately painted gourds.

Casita de la Musica

Av 5 between Av Juárez and C 2. Pick up the latest Mexican pop hits here, or browse a decent selection of more traditional Yucatecan *trova* ballads and folk music from around Mexico.

Idé

Av 5 at C 16. This small, spare shop specializes in creative, modern jewellery incorporating semiprecious stones, particularly opals. Definitely pricier than other silver vendors, but the intricate work is unique and done on the premises.

Juan's Hammocks

Av 10 between Av Juárez and C 2, next to Roger's Boots. At first glance this small shack, which doubles as a money exchange, doesn't look promising, but it's a great source for well-priced, good-quality hammocks, available in a rainbow of tightly woven col-

ourful nylon threads. The owner also stocks a few thick-string cheapies – pass on these, as they're uncomfortable and won't hold their shape.

Maya Art

Av 5 between C 6 and C 8. Nestled in a small garden courtyard (look for the stained-glass "El Jardín de Marieta" sign), this excellent gallery is packed with comical and grotesque wood masks, folk paintings and, best of all, beautiful antique *huipiles*, the intricately embroidered Mayan women's smocks. The latter are expensive, but a good piece shows a level of craftsmanship that's no longer made today for any price.

Paseo del Carmen

Av 5 at C 1 Sur. Major attractions at this stylish open-air mall are hip Euro labels like Custo Barcelona and Bershka, as well as a few cool bars and lounges, such as *Narguila*, which serves up cocktails and Middle Eastern water pipes, and Havana import *La Bodeguita del Medio*, which specializes in mojitos. Rough-hewn rock fountains and whitewashed stucco create an environment pleasant even for non-shoppers.

Pygmees

Av 5 between C 8 and C 10. A funky clothing, accessories and house-wares store featuring whimsical kids' outfits from French label Poudre de Perlimpinpin and bright asymmetrical women's cotton clothing. The colour-block lightning-bolt miniskirt is the perfect Playa item.

Qué Pequeño es el Mundo

C 1 Sur between Av 20 and Av 25. A welcome addition to the Playa community, this well-stocked bookstore is run by a friendly and informed staff quick to make recommendations on English and Spanish titles alike. Come here to stock up on Mayan and Mexican history, or just for a riveting beach novel.

Cafés

Café Sasta

Av 5 between C 8 and C 10. The sidewalk tables at this Italian coffeehouse are an ideal spot for watching the fashion parade on La Quinta at all hours, while pastries and espresso are the main dining attractions.

Carmencita

Av 5 at C 20. An Argentine café where the mod, green-lit decor out front belies a traditional kitchen in the back. Empanadas grace the menu, along with hearty sandwiches like grilled steak or chorizo with *chimichurri*.

La Cueva del Chango

C 38 between Av 5 and the beach. Closes at 2pm on Sun. With tables scattered in a big garden filled with birds and a little stream, this outdoor restaurant is a local favourite for long, very late breakfasts (till 5pm), and the perfect destination after a morning stroll up the beach. The menu includes tasty empanadas and crepes with honey, starting at around $4, and house-roasted coffee.

La Floresta

West side of Hwy-307 just north of Av Juárez. This big palapa next to the highway is a road-tripper's delight, serving delicious over-stuffed *tacos de camarón* ($1.20

▼CAFÉ SASTA

▲BABE'S

each), the perfect marriage of batter-fried shrimp, mayo and chunky tomato salsa. For a bit of variety, seafood cocktails and ceviches are available too, starting at $6.

Hot

C 10 between Av 5 and Av 10. A bakery and small café serving fresh muffins, bagels and brownies as well as giant cinnamon rolls. Those with heartier appetites can choose from omelettes and sandwiches, as well as eggs Benedict on the weekends. Another branch is on Calle 12 north of Avenida 5.

El Oasis

C 12 between Av 5 and Av 10. Closed Sun. While the original *El Oasis* earned its reputation selling shrimp tacos out by the highway, this cosy new branch has a fuller menu of seafood dishes for $6 and up. The tacos ($1.20 each) aren't quite as good as *La Floresta*'s, but they're the best you can get around the central tourist strip.

Pan de Carmen

Av Juárez at Av 10. Pick up inexpensive bread, sweet and savoury *hojaldres* (filled puff pastry) and *pan dulce* at this fragrant Mexican bakery that's usually well stocked throughout the day.

Restaurants

100% Natural

Av 5 between C 10 and C 12. As with the Cancún branch, Playa's outpost serves fresh, often vegetarian Mexican food – lighter versions of enchiladas and fajitas – along with big sandwiches and fresh fruit juices. Not the cheapest, but reliably good and set in a big garden.

Los Almendros

Av 10 at C 6. A traditional Mexican restaurant with an outdoor grill, *Los Almendros* is unpretentious and reasonably priced, with delicious tacos and a daily *comida corrida* (set menu) that's available for both lunch and dinner for just $3.50.

Babe's

C 10 between Av 5 and Av 10. This Swedish-owned Thai noodle house typifies Playa's international hodgepodge – and the mojitos aren't bad either. Dishes like pad thai start at about $4.50.

▲ MEDIA LUNA

Buenos Aires

Av 5 between C 4 and C 6 ☏984/873-2751. Set back in an alley, this fairly authentic Argentine steakhouse is the best place in town for grilled meat, with thick-cut steaks from $15.

El Faisán y El Venado

C 2 just east of Hwy-307. Very well-priced Yucatecan specialities such as *panuchos* (crisp-fried tortillas topped with shredded turkey) and *carne ahumada* (smoked pork in a citrus marinade) are the draw at this sprawling family restaurant that bustles at lunch.

John Gray's Place

C Corazón, north of Av 5 between C 12 and C 14. Chef John Gray's excellent restaurant in Puerto Morelos recently opened this new branch in Playa, with the same varied, tasty menu (including enormous spinach salads and grilled fish with mango salsa) served in the second-floor dining room. One improvement on the original place: the cosy bar and lounge – try the signature "smoky margarita" made with mezcal.

Media Luna

Av 5 between C 12 and C 14. Eclectic veggie and seafood restaurant – think *chiles rellenos* presented as a lasagna ($8) – with a well-priced lunch special, big healthy sandwiches ($7 and up) and delicious breakfasts of fruit salad, French toast and pancakes ($5 and up).

El Olivo

Av 10 between C 6 and C 8. A charming shoebox-size tapas bar, complete with mini portions of *tortilla española* (potato omelette) as well as savoury seafood snacks, all starting at just $3 per plate.

Osteria La Rucola

C 26 between Av 5 and Av 10 ☏984/879-3359. Closed Wed. A little patch of northern Italy in a quiet Playa Norte block, with dishes like an excellent octopus and arugula salad ($7) and handmade pasta with rosemary, shrimp and black olives ($9).

La Tarraya

Seafront at C 2. This Playa del Carmen institution has been holding its own against development for more than twenty years, serving standard beach fare like ceviches and *frito pescado* ($9 per kilo) with plenty of cold beer.

Yaxche

C 8 between Av 5 and Av 10 ☎984/873-2502. Haute Mayan is the agenda at this gracious restaurant with a pretty back garden: hot peppers stuffed with *cochinita pibil* (shredded roast pork), a Yucatecan shrimp gratin or lobster flambéed in *xtabentun*, a local liqueur. With entrées between $12 and $20, it's very reasonably priced, considering the lavish service and artful presentation. And just because it's fancy doesn't mean it's not spicy.

Bars

Bar Ranita

C 10 between Av 5 and Av 10. This snug and mellow wood-panelled room is populated by a crew of regulars – mostly expats – hanging out at the horseshoe-shaped bar. A welcome break from Playa's generally top-volume bar scene.

Capitán Tutix

On the beach at C 4 ☎984/803-1595. *The* pick-up joint in town, a jam-packed bar and disco with live music every night (10pm–midnight, no cover) and a predominantly young party crowd. For the after-party, the trance-heavy *Lumpax* next door takes over when *Tutix* closes its doors.

Dragon Bar

On the beach at C 12. Open until 4am. This open-air bar in the *Blue Parrot* hotel was once legendary, but now isn't too

distinct from other places with tables on the sand and swings in lieu of barstools. Nonetheless, it's friendly and has a popular happy hour (5–8pm), with live music in the afternoons and assorted dancers and fire-spinners at night.

Kartabar

C 12 at Av 1 ☎984/873-2228, ⊛www.kartabar.com. A stylish lounge, all black and white with enormous candles, that serves up Lebanese finger food, loads of cocktails and the obligatory belly dancer. The crowd is very high-society Playa.

El Tigre

Av 10 between C 2 and C 4. Good local spot for beers, ceviches and ridiculously generous *botanas* (free snacks). Women will probably feel more comfortable accompanied by a man; the billiards area upstairs is men-only. Closes by late afternoon.

Ula-Gula

Av 5 at C 10. This small candlelit bar on a corner of La Quinta is a prime vantage point for people-watching, and a DJ usually provides a cool house soundtrack. The restaurant upstairs is uneven, but the simpler dishes are delicious.

Clubs

Alux

Av Juárez, 400m west of Hwy-307 ☎984/803-0713. This club is a trek from the main drag – tell the cab driver "ah-LOOSH" – but deserves a visit for its unique setting inside a large cave. Dinner of rich (if somewhat overpriced) French-tropical dishes begins at 8pm; a DJ or a floor show of belly dancers and jazz musicians gets started around 10pm. Usually no cover, but drinks are $7 and up.

Mambo Café
C 6 between Av 5 and Av 10 ☎984/803-2656. Closed Mon. An outpost of the popular Cancún club, this space is similarly professional, with excellent sound and a roster of big-name Cuban and Dominican bands. Wednesday is ladies night, with open bar from 10pm till midnight. Cover is usually $5.

La Santanera
C 14 between Av 5 and Av 10. Super-stylish club with international DJ cred, a comfortable, breezy lounge area, cool global house and ambient music and deliciously strong drinks. The scantily clad party crowd – equal parts tourists and residents – usually staggers out at around 5am.

Isla Cozumel

A forty-kilometre-long island directly off the coast of Playa del Carmen, Isla Cozumel is one of the world's foremost diving destinations. The spectacular coral reefs that ring much of the western and southern shore have been dazzling visitors since Jacques Cousteau first brought them to international attention in the 1960s – they're now a national marine park. More recently, the island has become a popular port of call for cruise ships, welcoming enormous vessels almost daily. The lone town, bustling San Miguel, has given over much of its waterfront to duty-free jewellery stores and giant souvenir marts, though it is more diverse – and affordable – farther inland. When the crowds prove too much, the sprawling, overgrown ruins at San Gervasio in the middle of island or the windswept eastern coast, with its deserted beaches and pounding waves, both provide an alluring respite.

San Miguel

On the west coast, San Miguel is the island's only major population centre and home to about 85,000 people. It's a clean, cheerful place, a bit sprawling with big blocks and low buildings – a few of which are little Caribbean-style clapboard houses that have somehow resisted decades of heavy rains and glaring sun. The main square, the Plaza del Sol, is directly opposite the ferry dock and acts as the hub of activity for visitors, and for *cozumeleños* on Sunday evenings, when everyone comes out to listen to music and chat. Many stroll along the wide seafront avenue, Avenida Rafael Melgar, which is graced with large statues commemorating Cozumel's Mayan cultural heritage and long tradition of fishing. From there, the town fans out for many blocks more than tourists will see; the downtown area, from the seafront to Avenida 30 (also called Avenida Coldwell), holds all the

Visiting Isla Cozumel

If you arrive at the **airport** north of San Miguel, a **shared van** service runs into town for about $4, or you can take a taxi directly to your hotel, starting at $9.

Two **ferries** make the half-hour trip from Playa del Carmen on the hour between 6am and midnight. The prices are the same ($9 one way, or $12.50 for a same-day return), but Mexico Waterjets, departing from the pier at Calle 1 Sur, provides faster, more comfortable service. (The other pier, for Ultramar boats, is at the end of Avenida Constituyentes.)

A helpful **tourist office** (Mon–Sat 8.30am–5pm ☎987/869-0212, ✉turismoczm @yahoo.com.mx) is located on Avenida Melgar at the ferry pier in a kiosk immediately south of the boardwalk.

PLACES

Isla Cozumel

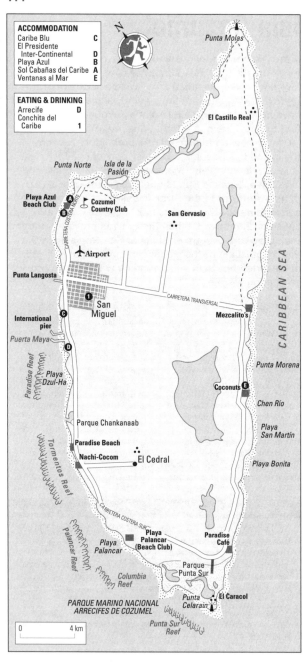

ACCOMMODATION
Caribe Blu   C
El Presidente
  Inter-Continental   D
Playa Azul   B A
Sol Cabañas del Caribe   A
Ventanas al Mar   E

EATING & DRINKING
Arrecife   D
Conchita del
  Caribe   1

Punta Molas

El Castillo Real

Punta Norte   Isla de la
               Pasión

Playa Azul
Beach Club   A
               B   Cozumel
                    Country Club

San Gervasio

✈ Airport

Punta Langosta

1   San
     Miguel   CARRETERA TRANSVERSAL

International   Mezcalito's
pier   C
Puerta Maya
              D

Paradise Reef   CARIBBEAN SEA

              Playa
              Dzul-Ha   Punta Morena

                                    Coconuts E

Parque Chankanaab   Chen Río

Tormentos Reef   Playa
                                                 San Martín
Paradise Beach

Nachi-Cocom   El Cedral   Playa Bonita

              CARRETERA COSTERA SUR

                                                 Paradise
Playa   Playa   Café
Palancar   Palancar
Palancar Reef   (Beach Club)
                                      Parque
              Columbia   Punta Sur
              Reef
                                      Punta
PARQUE MARINO NACIONAL   Celarain   El Caracol
ARRECIFES DE COZUMEL

0   4 km   Punta Sur
                                      Reef

San Miguel's namesake

The town's name was chosen in the late 1800s, when the island's population grew with refugees from the bitter Caste Wars, when the Maya resisted control by central Mexico. As workers were breaking ground, they unearthed a large, richly adorned **statue** of Saint Michael. Research suggested that it dated from the early 1500s, when Spanish explorer **Juan de Grijalva** brought it to the island as a gift for the native Maya. The discovery inspired the townspeople to take San Miguel as their patron saint, and to build the **Iglesia de San Miguel** on the site where the statue was found, at the corner of Avenida Juárez and Avenida 10. The statue of the winged archangel brandishing his sword is still on display on the church altar.

necessary hotels, restaurants and services.

Museo de la Isla de Cozumel

Av Melgar between C 4 and C 6
☎987/872-0914. Daily 9am–5pm.
$5. A concise introduction to the primary points of Yucatán history, the small but well-organized San Miguel has exhibits on the island's indigenous flora and fauna, its famous reef systems and the history of the island from the Maya era to the present day. You'll also see a good collection of Maya artefacts and old photos showing Cozumel's exuberant Carnaval festivities. In the back on the ground floor is a traditional Maya hut, where an interesting local explains (primarily in Spanish) the uses of the various foodstuffs, herbs and accoutrements lying about. The museum occasionally hosts live music and theatre events – check with the tourist office (see box, p.113).

Mercado Municipal

Av Salas between Av 20 and Av 25.
Daily 7am–4pm. Coming from the T-shirt shops and tequila bars ringing the Plaza del Sol, San Miguel's central market seems to be in an entirely different town. This block of orderly little stalls, tucked under a high tin roof, is a welcome reminder of the thousands of people who live in San Miguel not necessarily engaged in the tourist trade. Along with heaps of fresh produce and rows of butcher stalls (not for the squeamish), you can find colourful, inexpensive kitchen equipment and a good selection of bargain lunch counters and juice bars.

▼MERCADO MUNICIPAL

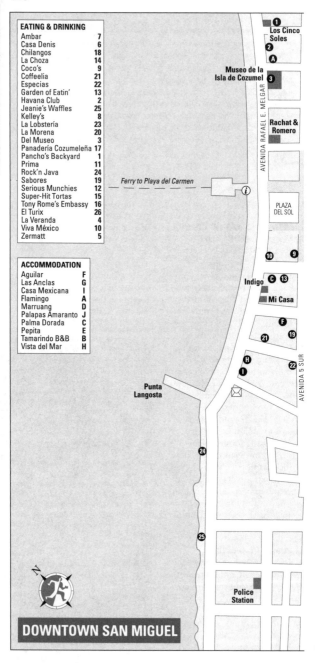

EATING & DRINKING

Ambar	7
Casa Denis	6
Chilangos	18
La Choza	14
Coco's	9
Coffeelia	21
Especias	22
Garden of Eatin'	13
Havana Club	2
Jeanie's Waffles	25
Kelley's	8
La Lobstería	23
La Morena	20
Del Museo	3
Panadería Cozumeleña	17
Pancho's Backyard	1
Prima	11
Rock'n Java	24
Sabores	19
Serious Munchies	12
Super-Hit Tortas	15
Tony Rome's Embassy	16
El Turix	26
La Veranda	4
Viva México	10
Zermatt	5

ACCOMMODATION

Aguilar	F
Las Anclas	G
Casa Mexicana	I
Flamingo	A
Marruang	D
Palapas Amaranto	J
Palma Dorada	C
Pepita	E
Tamarindo B&B	B
Vista del Mar	H

Los Cinco Soles

Museo de la Isla de Cozumel

AVENIDA RAFAEL E. MELGAR

Rachat & Romero

Ferry to Playa del Carmen

PLAZA DEL SOL

Indigo

Mi Casa

AVENIDA 5 SUR

Punta Langosta

Police Station

DOWNTOWN SAN MIGUEL

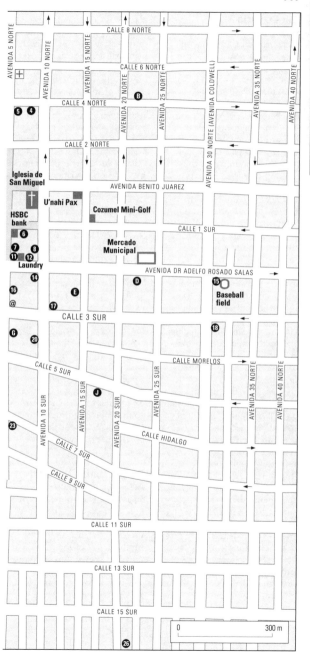

CALLE 8 NORTE

AVENIDA 5 NORTE
AVENIDA 10 NORTE
AVENIDA 15 NORTE
AVENIDA 20 NORTE

CALLE 6 NORTE

B

AVENIDA 25 NORTE
AVENIDA 30 NORTE (AVENIDA COLDWELL)
AVENIDA 35 NORTE
AVENIDA 40 NORTE

CALLE 4 NORTE

5 **4**

CALLE 2 NORTE

Iglesia de
San Miguel

AVENIDA BENITO JUAREZ

U'nahi Pax

Cozumel Mini-Golf

HSBC
bank

6

CALLE 1 SUR

7 **8**
11 **12**
Laundry

Mercado
Municipal

14

AVENIDA DR ADELFO ROSADO SALAS

16
@

E

D

15
Baseball
field

17

CALLE 3 SUR

G

20

18

CALLE 5 SUR

CALLE MORELOS

AVENIDA 35 NORTE
AVENIDA 40 NORTE

AVENIDA 10 SUR
AVENIDA 15 SUR

J

AVENIDA 20 SUR
AVENIDA 25 SUR

CALLE 7 SUR

CALLE HIDALGO

23

CALLE 9 SUR

CALLE 11 SUR

CALLE 13 SUR

CALLE 15 SUR

0   300 m

26

San Gervasio

Midway across the island on the Carretera Transversal, then 6km north. Daily 7am–5pm. $5. The largest excavated Maya site on the island, the city of San Gervasio was built to honour Ixchel, goddess of fertility and weaving, and became one of the most important pilgrimage destinations in Central America. The city was also part of a larger trading community on the Yucatán coast – along with Tulum (see p.131) and El Rey in Cancún (see p.56) – that flourished until about 1600. Today, though, the ruins are not all that impressive, but, as they are part of a larger nature reserve, they're worth a visit for their scenic jungle setting. Early mornings or late afternoons reveal numerous bird species, butterflies and other wildlife. The central portions of the city are modelled on Chichén Itzá, with several small plazas connected by *sacbeob*, or long white roads paved with limestone.

One of the first buildings you reach is the Estructura Manitas, a small residential building decorated with red handprints. This is a somewhat common motif at other Maya sites, but its significance is still not understood. To the right, Chichan Nah is a dwarfish building probably used for ceremonial purposes, as it is similar to the miniature temples at Tulum. By contrast, Structure 31, off to the left, is a large residential building with a portico. In the later centuries, it was probably the seat of the *halach uinic*, the ruler of Cozumel, just one of many independent statelets in the Yucatán after the fall of centralized power in Chichén Itzá. The main cluster of buildings, arranged around a compact plaza, was the central administrative area. Five hundred metres northwest along a *sacbé* lies the principal shrine to Ixchel, the Ka'na Nah. The tallest pyramid on the site (though still not towering), it features a few remnants of painted stucco adornments. Down the northeast *sacbé*, marked by a delicate arch, is the Post-Classic Nohoch Nah temple and the much older Casa de los Murciélagos; construction on the latter started as early as 700 AD.

El Cedral

Carretera Costera Sur Km 17.5, then 3km inland. This tiny village, founded in 1847, is now primarily a rustic vacation spot for San Miguel's better-off denizens. With its small Maya site near a modern Spanish church filled with folk art, it can provide a pleasant stop on an island tour. Or stay to visit several small cenotes nearby – they're best reached on horseback (inquire with guides at the ruins). In late April and early May, the village hosts the ten-day-long Fiesta de la Santa Cruz, a huge fair commemorating the meeting of Maya and Spanish cultures with bullfights, prize-winning livestock and dancing.

Parque Marino Nacional Arrecifes de Cozumel

$5 park fee. The boundaries of Cozumel's vast marine reserve encompass the beaches and most of the reefs edging the southern half of the island. The coral has grown into steep drop-offs, massive towers and deep canyons, as well as some beautiful shallow gardens. At the more remote reefs, you can see larger pelagic fish and occasionally dolphins. Regulations require that you be accompanied by a licensed dive guide; expect the park fee to be tacked on to any organized diving or snorkelling trip you make.

On the western, leeward side, a steady current typically runs south to north, making for easy drift dives and snorkelling. Perhaps the best spot for both diving and snorkelling is Palancar Shallows, about 2km off the southwest coast, an area that ranges from five-metre-deep gardens to a mini-wall dropping 18m. The main strip reef is riddled with fissures and caves, providing nooks for all kinds of sea life as well as shelter from currents. You'll see Cozumel's famous (and rare) black coral as well as giant stove-pipe and tube sponges that harbour brilliantly coloured fish. The other sections of the five-kilometre-long Palancar Reef are accessible to divers only, but equally fascinating – Palancar Deep in particular stands up to repeat visits.

A bit to the south, Colombia Shallows is the farthest trip most day boats make from San Miguel. Although it is only 10m at its deepest, this sprawling coral garden impresses seasoned divers and snorkellers alike. Sediment-rich runoff from the mangroves in Laguna Colombia help feed the thriving ecosystem of tall coral towers studded with vibrant sponges and anemones punctuate the floor, and meadows of sea grass are spawning grounds for a dazzling variety of fish. Rays frequent the area, as do nurse sharks and eels.

At Punta Sur, directly south from Laguna Colombia, strong currents (and an hour-long boat ride) deter all but the strongest divers. Those who undertake the journey are rewarded with a dramatic network of deep caverns and fissures – the largest are known as the Cathedral and the Devil's Throat – completely encrusted with vibrant corals and thronged with fish.

Playa Azul Beach Club

Carretera Costera Norte Km 4 just north of *Playa Azul* hotel. Daily 10am–5pm. This gem of a beach is the best option close to San Miguel, with clean sand, a little rocky spot for snorkelling and clear, calm water that's good for swimming. The club is relatively empty on weekdays, but on Sunday afternoons it's the place to come if you want to hang out with locals, as the restaurant and playground get packed with families on their day off. You can also windsurf here and rent kayaks (about $10 per hour).

Dzul-Ha

Carretera Costera Sur Km 6.8 ☎987/872-5877, ✉dzulha@hotmail .com. Mon–Sat 8am–5pm, Sun 9am–5pm. Dive shop closed Sun. The coral gardens here are lush and very close to shore, making this the island's easiest and best spot for wade-in snorkelling. You can rent gear from the dive shop at the beach bar, which also has tasty, reasonably priced food. The sea and beach are too rocky for actual swimming and lounging, so you're better off paying the $5 drink minimum to use the pool.

Parque Chankanaab

Carretera Costera Sur Km 9 ☎987/872-0914. Daily 7am–5pm. $10. The beautiful Laguna Chankanaab is this national park's centrepiece, full of turtles and lurid parrotfish. There's also plenty of beach for lounging, or botanical gardens, dolphin swims and mini golf for the more active. A dive shop caters

Isla Cozumel **PLACES**

▲EL CARACOL RUIN, PARQUE PUNTA SUR

to those who want to explore the reef beyond the lagoon, but anyone but beginners will probably enjoy the island's other dive spots more. Unfortunately, a small asphalt spill in June 2004 damaged some of the reef here and at Playa Corona to the south; cleanup is underway. Like the big eco-parks on the mainland, Chankanaab feels slightly overdeveloped, and it can get very crowded on cruise-ship days, but it's a great option for families, with a protected children's beach.

Paradise Beach

Carretera Costera Sur Km 14.5 ☎987/871-9010, ⊛www .paradise-beach-cozumel.net. Daily 9am–6pm. The western coast's newest beach club offers free use of beach chairs, kayaks, snorkel gear and floating water toys moored offshore. The three bars (a central one, an upstairs deck with a view, and an outpost down the beach) serve deluxe umbrella drinks. If the cruise-ship crowds get heavy, the now less popular *Playa San Francisco* club next door usually has more room.

Nachi-Cocom

Carretera Costera Sur Km 16.5. Daily 9am–5pm. For those willing to pay (no cover, but a $10 minimum per person at the club's restaurant), Nachi-Cocom offers a more serene beach experience than some other west-coast clubs, as it's barely known among cruise-shippers and caters to well-heeled island residents. Fronted by shallow water, the beautiful beach is the setting for very well-kept facilities, including changing rooms and an enormous swimming pool and Jacuzzi – but note that there's no snorkelling here.

Playa Palancar

Carretera Costera Sur Km 19. Daily 9am–6pm. Well toward the southern end of the island, this is the least crowded of the leeward beaches, with a laid-back atmosphere to match. There's no entertainment other than eating at the restaurant, which serves seafood specialities like *tikin-xic* (fish baked with *achiote* in banana leaves, $10). From here you can also arrange a boat ride out to Palancar Reef just offshore.

Parque Punta Sur

Carretera Costera Sur Km 27
☎987/872-0914. Daily 9am–5pm.
$10. At Cozumel's southernmost
point, this reserve protects a
diverse range of wildlife, from
endangered sea turtles to the
swallows that gave the island
its name: *cuzamil* means "place
of the swallows" in Maya. The
2750-acre site contains a large
network of lagoons, several
lovely beaches and mangrove
swamps that host a number of
migratory bird species, such as
roseate spoonbills, giant frigates
and various herons, as well as
four endemic ones, including
the vibrant Cozumel emerald
and the Cozumel thrasher, until
recently suspected to be extinct.

A creaking wood-sided truck
transports visitors around the
sights (or you can rent bicycles
or electric buggies), including a
beach restaurant serving good
fried fish, viewing towers and the
Templo El Caracol – which may
have been built by the Maya as
an ancient lighthouse – where
you can hear the wind whistling
through the conch shells embed-
ded in its walls. Nearby is the
modern Punta Celerain lighthouse, which you can climb to
the top of the modern lighthouse
for amazing views. Installed in
the former lighthouse-keeper's
house is the small Museo de la
Navegación (daily 10am–4pm),
which has a series of interesting
displays on maritime history on
the Yucatán coast.

For an additional fee, you can
arrange a small-group night
tour of the crocodile or sea
turtle reserve areas and scientific
monitoring stations (details at
the park entrance).

The eastern coast

Cozumel's wild eastern shoreline
remains undeveloped because it
faces the open sea, and in most
places the water is too rough
for swimming. The twenty-
kilometre stretch of highway
along the island's southeastern
edge is a beautiful drive and a
refreshing contrast to the busier
west coast. Along the way you'll
pass tantalizing deserted beaches
– though swim only where
you see others, and be wary

▼MEZCALITO'S BEACH BAR

of strong currents – and the occasional no-frills beach bar, open only till sundown because there's no electricity. The first of these as you arrive via the cross-island road, and generally the most crowded as it's right at the intersection, is *Mezcalito's*. The beach here is big and deep and the party atmosphere strong; ATV tours to El Castillo Real, an unremarkable ruin, depart from here and head north on an extremely rocky track (do not attempt this in a rental car).

Heading south on the coastal highway, you'll eventually reach Punta Morena, home to a small surfer scene. Shortly after is *Coconuts* restaurant and bar, which offers a striking view from a tall bluff; the beach below is usually empty. Chen Río, a little farther on, has a protected cove where you can swim and snorkel (bring your own gear), and the bar serves great margaritas. The relatively serene Playa San Martín, just south, has no services, but flags mark the day's swimming conditions. Past a rocky point, Playa Bonita has another beach club – the water is shallow and umbrellas are for rent. Finally, the road turns inland at the entrance to Parque Punta Sur, and the *Paradise Café*, known for its all-reggae soundtrack and savoury shrimp quesadillas, marks the junction.

▼SCUBA TRAINING AREA, CARIBE BLU

Accommodation

Aguilar

C 3 Sur 98, between Av Melgar and Av 5 Sur, San Miguel ☎987/872-0307, Ⓦwww.cozumel-hotels.net/aguilar. Quiet, slightly kitsch rooms with no shortage of plastic flowers. All rooms have a/c and are set away from the road around a garden with a small pool. The location is convenient, and scooter and car hire are available. Doubles from $44.

Las Anclas

Av 5 Sur 325, between C 3 and C 5, San Miguel ☎987/872-5476, Ⓦwww.lasanclas.com. A handful of well-designed two-storey suites with kitchenettes, all spotless and perfectly maintained; with a queen-size bed upstairs and two day-beds downstairs, they sleep up to four. A little shared garden makes the place feel extra homey. Rough Guides readers receive a 10 percent discount on the standard rate of $90.

Caribe Blu

Costera Sur Km 2.2 ☎987/872-0188, Ⓦwww.caribeblu.net. Basic but comfortable divers' hotel very close to town with an excellent shop, Blue Angel, and shallow training area right off the small beach out front. All rooms have sea views and private balconies, and there's a pool. Non-guests are welcome to snorkel off the pier. Doubles from $75.

Casa Mexicana

Av Melgar 457, between C 5 and C 7, San Miguel ☎987/872-9090, ⊛www .casamexicanacozumel.com. Stylish hotel on the seafront road, with a pool, travel agency, business centre and gym. The ninety rooms are slick and modern, with cable TV, marble baths and balconies. Buffet breakfast is included. Doubles from $110.

Flamingo

C 6 Norte between Av Melgar and Av 5 Sur, San Miguel ☎987/872-1264, ⊛www.hotelflamingo.com. Fun hotel popular with the scuba set, with a rooftop terrace and bar and a Cuban-fusion restaurant that also hosts live salsa bands. Guests can use the beach up the coast at *Playa Azul*; well-priced dive packages are an option. Doubles from $69.

Marruang

Av Salas 440, between Av 20 and Av 25, San Miguel ☎987/872-1678. A bargain option for those who want to get well away from San Miguel's tourist centre: rooms are clean, with TVs and firm mattresses, and you can start the morning with snacks from the market directly across the street. Doubles from $20.

Palapas Amaranto

C 5 Sur between Av 15 and Av 20, San Miguel ☎987/872-3219, ⊛www .amarantobb.com. Winding staircases and curving walls distinguish these three fanciful round stucco palapas and two apartments stacked in a tile-trimmed tower. Rooms – all with fridge and microwave, and most with a/c – are clustered around a cosy courtyard and

▲LOBBY, CASA MEXICANA

small pool. If arriving in the afternoon, check in or inquire at *Tamarindo*. Rooms from $45.

Palma Dorada

Av Salas 44, between Av Melgar and Av 5, San Miguel ☎987/872-0330, ⊛pdinn@prodigy.net.mx. Chummy service complements the cheery, tidy rooms done up with bright colours and an airy rooftop lounge. A few suites with kitchenettes are available. Doubles from $30; $43 with a/c.

Pepita

Av 15 Sur 120, at C 1 Sur, San Miguel ☎987/872-0098. By far the best of the budget options, with proud owners and two storeys of clean, attractive rooms with a/c and TV ringing a large, pretty courtyard. Complimentary coffee in the mornings. Doubles from $30.

Playa Azul

Carretera Costera Norte Km 4 ☎987/872-0043, ⊛www .playa-azul.com. At this swanky little resort on the best stretch

PLACES Isla Cozumel

of beach north of town, the fifty ocean-view rooms are tastefully decorated with wicker furniture and tile floors. There are several bars and restaurants, a spa and gym; the pool is a bit small, however. Golf and dive packages are available, and rates dip sharply in low season. Doubles from $185.

El Presidente Inter-Continental

Carretera Costera Sur Km 6.5 ☎987/872-9500, ⊛www.cozumel .interconti.com. The sharp-edged Sixties modernist design of Cozumel's first luxury hotel can feel a little austere, but the setting is flawless, with both a fine protected beach and good snorkelling off a long pier. All rooms have ocean views, and the new spa offers lavish beauty treatments. Doubles from $240.

Sol Cabañas del Caribe

Carretera Costera Norte Km 5.1 ☎987/872-0017, ⊛www.solmelia.com. This small resort is showing its age with its rather dated decor, but it's very mellow and quiet, with just 39 simply furnished rooms and nine private cottages facing the water. You can snorkel right off the dock. Doubles from $90; cottages from $120.

▲PLAYA AZUL RESORT

Tamarindo

C 4 Norte 421, between Av 20 and Av 25, San Miguel ☎987/872-6190, ⊛www.tamarindobb.com. A sociable French-Mexican couple have put a distinctive stamp on their place: his architectural skills created pretty rooms with cosy nooks and whimsically placed windows; her cooking and island expertise put guests at ease. Two of the five rooms share a

▼EL PRESIDENTE INTERCONTINENTAL

kitchen; a/c is available in two others. There's also a big yard and outdoor grill. Full breakfast included. Rooms from $38.

Ventanas al Mar
On the east coast 5km south of Mezcalito's ⊛www.cozumel-hotels.net/ventanas-al-mar. This full-service hotel – the only one on the eastern coast – opened in 2004 as a fully wind-powered escape. Bring groceries: there are no services on this side, but the gigantic rooms all have kitchenettes, as well as terraces overlooking the crashing surf. Guests get discounts at *Coconuts* restaurant next door, and rates include full breakfast. Doubles from $79.

Vista del Mar
Av Melgar 45, between C 5 and C 7, San Miguel ☎987/872-0545, ⊛www.hotelvistadelmar.com. This small hotel is done up in earth tones and natural fibres. Front rooms have an ocean view at the price of street noise; back rooms have views of the big Jacuzzi. Continental breakfast is included. Good value for this level of comfort and design, with doubles from $66.

Shops

Los Cinco Soles
Av Melgar at C 8 Norte, San Miguel. A vast handicrafts superstore with more tasteful items than other giant tourist shops. Smaller, standard-issue souvenirs are overpriced, but the selection of jewellery and housewares – including elegant, modern pewter serving bowls and lead-free dishes – is excellent. A related store, Mi Casa, on Avenida Melgar near C 3, has a larger selection of home decor items.

Indigo
Av Melgar between C 3 and Av Salas, San Miguel. A tiny but richly stocked storefront selling antique embroidery from around Latin America, as well as Cuban cigars. Beautiful work, if expensive.

Rachat & Romero
Av Melgar at C 2, San Miguel. Of the seemingly endless parade of jewellers along the seafront, Rachat & Romero distinguishes itself with the most varied selection of loose gems and semiprecious stones.

U'nahi Pax
Av Juárez at Av 15, San Miguel. Every Mexican musical instrument imaginable, from pre-Columbian drums and rattles to elaborate harps and big-bellied guitars, is in stock here, along with a good selection of folk music on CD.

▼U'NAHI PAX

Cafés

Chilangos

Av 30 (Coldwell) between C 3 Sur and C Morelos, San Miguel. Closed Sun. *Huaraches*, big, open-face tortillas ($1.50 each), are the house speciality at this popular dinnertime snack bar; select your own combination of toppings, such as cheese and *nopales* (cactus strips).

Coco's

Av 5 no. 180, between C 1 and Av Salas, San Miguel. Tues–Sun 6am–noon. At this Cozumel institution, you get American diner style – complete with chatty waitresses, free coffee refills and Formica tables – with Mexican breakfast standards like eggs with *mole* ($4.50). The cinnamon rolls are satisfyingly gooey.

Coffeelia

C 5 Sur 85, between Av Melgar and Av 5, San Miguel. A local owner pre-

▼COFFEELIA

sides over her homely kitchen in this sweet café with room to lounge outdoors. The menu mixes fresh Mexican dishes, fruit smoothies and huge Dutch-style pancakes ($4.50 and up). Breakfast is served all day; in the evening, you might catch a singer or a storyteller.

Del Museo

Av Melgar between C 4 and C 6, at the Museo de la Isla de Cozumel, San Miguel. Mon–Sat 7am–2pm. Enjoy a quiet breakfast or lunch on the upstairs balcony of the city museum. The view of the sea is impressive, the coffee is spiked with cinnamon, and the food – from *huevos rancheros* to club sandwiches (both about $5) – is fresh and filling.

Garden of Eatin'

Av Salas between Av Melgar and Av 5, San Miguel. Vegetarians will rejoice at the sprawling, sparkling-clean salad bar and the tasty sandwiches, ranging from falafel to imaginative combos involving pesto and sprouts, for about $5.

Jeanie's Waffles

Av Melgar at C 11 Sur, San Miguel. Daily 6am–3pm. "La Casa del Waffle" is a popular breakfast and lunch option, not just for its giant waffles, but also for its sandwiches and substantial fruit salads, served at tables on the sand.

Panadería Cozumeleña

Entrance on C 3 at Av 10, San Miguel. Stop by this sweet-smelling bakery to pick up *pan dulce* to go, or, for a leisurely light breakfast, settle in at the adjacent coffee shop and neighbourhood hangout (entrance on the corner).

▲SUPER HIT TORTAS

Rock'n Java

Av Melgar 602, between C 7 and C 11, San Miguel ☎ 987/872-4405. Mon–Fri 7am–11pm, Sat 7am–2pm. Healthy sandwiches, salads and veggie chile (all between $4 and $8) are balanced out by fantastically rich and delicious desserts, such as German chocolate cake, at this American-owned seafront diner. Delivery is available to hotels south of town.

Serious Munchies

Av Salas between Av 5 and Av 10, San Miguel. Daily noon–11pm. Giant sandwiches ($3–5) are the main attraction here, ranging from cheese and avocado to big and messy meatball – or you can opt for a veggie-heavy stir-fry. A good place to pick up snacks for a day-trip or picnic.

Super Hit Tortas

Av 30 at Av Salas, San Miguel. Meaty Mexican-style sandwiches with plenty of toppings for just $1.50; in the summer, they make an ideal snack before attending a baseball game at the field behind. There's another branch at Avenida 30 and Calle 15.

Zermatt

C 4 Norte at Av 5, San Miguel. Daily 7am–3pm. Swiss-owned bakery serving huge sugar doughnuts and flaky *palmiers*, alongside Mexican sweet treats like *cuernitas* (cinnamon-covered crescent rolls). Wash it all down with a strong espresso or cappuccino.

Restaurants

Casa Denis

C 1 between Av 5 and Av 10, San Miguel ☎987/872-0067. Open since 1945, *Casa Denis* occupies a little wood-frame house. Bigger meals like chicken enchiladas ($8 and up) can be bland, though the fare is better than any other plaza restaurant. The better way to go is a beer and some *panuchos* ($3.50) as you watch the action from your sidewalk table.

La Choza

Av Salas at Av 10, San Miguel. Busy and popular mid-price restaurant serving Mexican homestyle cooking. The daily lunch special isn't on the menu – ask the waiter, and you could get a rib-sticking meal for about $5. Entrées like fajitas and *pollo en relleno negro* (chicken in a black chile sauce) start at around $9.

Conchita del Caribe

Av 65 between C 21 and C 23, San Miguel. Closes at 6pm. Well off the tourist track in an unpromising-looking converted garage, this locally famous seafood spot is inexpensive and delicious – ceviches are particularly good ($7.50 for a generous "small" portion).

Especias

C 5 Sur at Av 10, San Miguel. Mon–Sat 5–10.30pm. Inexpensive Argentine, Mexican and even occasionally Thai meals ($3 for snacks like empanadas, about $7 for more substantial main dishes), served by an exceptionally hospitable husband and wife. The breezy dining room looks onto a small garden, a pleasant stop for an end-of-the-day beer – but beware of occasionally erratic opening hours.

La Lobstería

Av 5 at C 7, San Miguel. Closed Sun. As the name suggests, lobster

al gusto (choose from several classic preparations) is the main draw at this restaurant in a hundred-year-old palapa house. But the rest of the menu is equally appetizing, with each dish receiving a special touch: fish in a lively cilantro-mint salsa verde ($10), tamarind dressing on the big green salad. Excellent service too.

La Morena

Av 10 between C 3 and C 5, San Miguel. A family atmosphere with a gracious and accommodating owner, serving huge seafood platters for two ($35) as well as earthy seasonal specials like rich, walnut-based *chiles en nogada* ($7) and venison ($15).

Pancho's Backyard

Av Melgar 27 at C 8 Norte, San Miguel ☎987/872-2141. Closed for lunch Sat & Sun. By no means an "authentic" Mexican dining experience – especially at lunch, when it's a favorite with cruise-ship passengers – but easily the best service on the island, gracious to both big groups and solo diners. Very good margaritas, tortilla chips hot out of the deep-fryer, and

▼LA LOBSTERÍA

▲LA VERANDA

fresh-tasting, slightly dressed-up Mexican entrées ($10 and up for mains like shrimp with poblano peppers); the vegetarian selection is strong too.

Prima

Av Salas 109, between Av 5 and Av 10, San Miguel. Very popular (and very loud) restaurant with a rooftop terrace, serving decent pizza and classic Italian-American dishes like spaghetti with meat sauce ($7) and *fettucini alfredo* with shrimp ($10).

Sabores

Av 5 between C 3 Sur and C 5 Sur, San Miguel. Real home cooking: this lunch-only *cocina económica* is run out of the chef-owner's home. Just walk through the living room and kitchen and out to the huge shady garden, where you can choose from several entrées ($4.50, or a few dollars more for shrimp dishes). The set price includes soup and an all-you-can-drink jug of *agua de jamaica*. Everything is pre-pared individually and with care – don't miss it.

El Turix

Av 20 between C 17 and C 19, across from Corpus Christi church, San Miguel. Mon–Sat 6.30–11.30pm. Chef Rafael Ponce, originally from Mérida, has cooked as far afield as Montreal, but returned to Mexico to re-create traditional Yucatecan dishes like *cochinita pibil* (pit-roasted pork) as well as a great coconut pie. The restaurant is simple, with big wooden tables, and the prices are low – everything's less than $10.

La Veranda

C 4 Norte 140, between Av 5 and Av 10, San Miguel ☏987/872-4132. Dine inside at this elegant Caribbean-style house, or in the huge back garden – either way, it's worth a splurge. Entrées like jerk chicken ($14) are well prepared and presented with (sometimes overdone) flair, but service can suffer when it's crowded; reservations recommended.

Bars

Ambar

Av 5 141, between C 1 and Av Salas, San Miguel. Closed Sun. A little slice of Playa style in Cozumel, this candlelit lounge serves up cocktails with live DJ accompaniment. It's also a dinner option, with refined northern Italian food, such as spinach-and-ricotta ravioli in brandy sauce for $11.

Arrecife

Carretera Costera Sur Km 6.5, at *El Presidente Inter-Continental* ☎987/872-0322. The veranda bar at the island's ritziest hotel is an elegant spot for a cocktail while admiring the sunset over the white beach and turquoise sea.

Havana Club

Av Melgar between C 6 and C 8 (enter through the Diamonds International store), San Miguel. Ridiculously expensive but tasty mojitos ($8), and about the only place in town to sit on a balcony and watch the sunset. The clientele is cigar-puffing, old-hand divers with stories to tell.

Kelley's

Av 10 between Av Salas and C 1 Sur, San Miguel ☎987-800-4438. A big open-air bar where you might see your divemaster or tour guide in their off-hours. Very friendly, with a pool table and live music on Fridays. Also serves big, tasty portions of American food during the day.

Tony Rome's Embassy

Av 5 between Av Salas and C 3 Sur, San Miguel. A hilarious karaoke venue where the larger-than-life proprietor, a cheery showman and a consummate host, entertains the crowds nightly. Loads of campy fun, but better for drinks than dinner.

Clubs

Viva México

Av Melgar at Av Salas, San Miguel. The one big nightclub in town where locals and tourists meet, *Viva México* offers a very loud and lively mix of hip-hop with Latin and club hits, all in a second-floor palapa fronting the sea. Two-for-one drink specials to those who arrive on the early side (don't expect much of a scene before 11pm).

Tulum

One of the most visited Maya sites in the Yucatán along with Chichén Itzá, **Tulum** stands exquisitely poised on fifteen-metre-high cliffs above the impossibly blue Caribbean. The sea has been an equally powerful attraction: first to backpackers, who made the bargain beachfront cabañas legendary on the international travel circuit, and now to a larger set of visitors who value the luxe-meets-rough sensibility of the newer resorts. Hotels along the beach rely on solar panels, wind turbines and generators; most have power for only about six hours a day. The candlelit tranquillity and the lull of the crashing surf belie the increasing development along these 20km of white sand. The actual town of Tulum, a bit inland along Hwy-307 and about 1km south of the entrance to the ruins, provides all the basic tourist services. Both in town and on the beach, you'll find great restaurants that blend Mexican and European flavours. The town is also the place to line up a diving or snorkelling excursion to one of the nearby cenotes – several of the best on the peninsula are just a few kilometres away.

Tulum ruins

Entrance east of Hwy-307, first stoplight at the northern edge of Tulum town. Winter daily 7am–5pm, summer 8am–6pm. $3.70. On a sunny day, with the turquoise sea glittering behind the weather-beaten grey stones, the first view of Tulum can be quite breathtaking, despite the small scale

Visiting Tulum

Buses run hourly from Cancún ($6; 2hr) and Playa del Carmen ($3; 1hr). Arriving in Tulum can be confusing because the community has two distinct parts. Hwy-307 turns slightly inland here, and the village straddles it, but most hotels are on the sea. To reach them coming by car from the north, turn left at the second stoplight, dominated by a San Francisco de Asis supermarket, following signs for "Boca Paila–Punta Allen". It's 3km to the junction with the coast road, with about one-third of the hotels to the north and the remainder running south for about 9km. The **bus station** is 1km south of this intersection; cabs wait out front to take you to the beach hotels (from $5).

If you're going directly to the **ruins**, avoid backtracking by getting off the bus at the visitors' centre, which is at the northernmost stoplight, about 1km before you reach the centre of town.

An unofficial but helpful **tourist information office** dispenses maps and tips from a storefront 1km along the road between town and the beach. *The Weary Traveler* hostel, opposite the bus station, has the same maps, plus plenty of free advice for budget travellers.

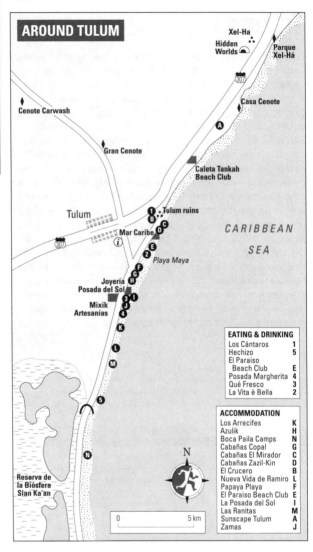

AROUND TULUM

Xel-Ha
Hidden Worlds
Parque Xel-Há

307

Casa Cenote

Cenote Carwash

A

Gran Cenote

Caleta Tankah
Beach Club

Tulum

1
B
Tulum ruins

D

Mar Caribe
i

E

2
Playa Maya

CARIBBEAN
SEA

F
G
H

Joyería
Posada del Sol

3 I
J
4

Mixik
Artesanías

K

L

M

5

N

Reserva de
la Bíosfera
Sian Ka'an

N

0   5 km

EATING & DRINKING

Los Cántaros	1
Hechizo	5
El Paraiso Beach Club	E
Posada Margherita	4
Qué Fresco	3
La Vita è Bella	2

ACCOMMODATION

Los Arrecifes	K
Azulik	H
Boca Paila Camps	N
Cabañas Copal	G
Cabañas El Mirador	C
Cabañas Zazil-Kin	D
El Crucero	B
Nueva Vida de Ramiro	L
Papaya Playa	F
El Paraiso Beach Club	E
La Posada del Sol	I
Las Ranitas	M
Sunscape Tulum	A
Zamas	J

of its buildings, all clustered in a compact mass within fortified walls. The city was built in the Late Post-Classic period, after 1200, and was still thriving when the Spanish first set eyes on the place in 1518. The entire site seems a bit haphazard because walls flare outward and doorways taper inward – not the effect of time, but an intentional design, and one that is echoed in other coastal sites such as El Rey in Cancún and San Gervasio on Cozumel. On the whole, the buildings seem less than grand when compared to the majestic Castillo at Chichén Itzá (see p.147).

Arrive in the early morning or late afternoon to avoid the worst crowds. The area is less than 500m long and takes only an hour or so to see, though you may want to allow time to swim at the tiny, perfect beach that punctuates the cliffs. A shuttle bus ($2) runs the 1km from the visitors' centre near the highway to the ticket kiosk and site entrance, which is through a breach in the wall that protected the city on three sides; the fourth faced the sea. This **wall**, some 5m high with a walkway along the top, may have had a defensive purpose, but more likely it delineated the ceremonial and administrative precinct – the site you see today – from nearby residential enclaves. In any case, the walls did take on a defensive role around 1890, when the site was reoccupied by Maya followers of the Talking Cross liberation movement, who practiced rituals here and held out against Mexican armies for more than 25 years.

Walking straight toward the sea from the entrance, you reach the **Casa del Cenote**, a square structure straddling a water-filled cave. A tomb occupies its central portion. On the bluff above and to the right are the **Templos Miniaturas**, several small-scale temples, complete with tiny lintels and moldings, that were probably used as shrines. Up the hill stands the **Templo del Díos del Viento** (Temple of the Wind God), a small, single-room structure on a round platform – a rare design for this region. Skirt the small beach to reach the north side of the main promontory and the **Templo del Díos**

Descendente. The diving (or descending) god, depicted here above the narrow entrance of the temple, is one of Tulum's quirks: the small, upside-down winged figure appears all over the city, but in only a handful of places elsewhere in the Mayan world. His exact meaning is unclear – he may represent the setting sun, or rain or lightning, or he may be the bee god, since honey was one of the Maya's most important exports. Immediately adjacent, the imposing **Castillo**, on the highest part of the site, commands fine views in every direction – but to protect the worn stones, visitors may now only look up at the building from the plaza at its base. The pyramid may have served not just as a temple, but also as a beacon or lighthouse – even without a light, it would have been an important landmark for mariners along an otherwise featureless coastline. Just south of the Castillo is the **Templo de la Estela** (Temple of the Stela), so called because in it was found a commemorative stone tablet bearing a date well before the foundation of the city (and presumably brought here from elsewhere).

Turning away from the sea, you face a cluster of buildings arranged on a city-like grid, with the chief structures set on stone platforms along parallel streets. The most fascinating of these – and what used to be the chief attraction here, before it was closed to visitors – is the **Templo de las Pinturas** (Temple of the Paintings). The murals – actually on the exterior of an older temple – have been preserved by the surrounding gallery you see now, decorated with masks of the rain god Chac. The predominant images are of Maya gods and symbols of nature's fertility: rain, maize and fish. One remarkable piece, done at a later date than the others, shows Chac seated on a four-legged animal – clearly inspired by the conquistadors with their horses.

Mar Caribe Beach Club

Left on the coast road, 2.3km north of the junction with the road to Tulum town. This beach is dotted with the boats of the fishing co-operative that runs the restaurant here – popular with locals on the weekends, who come for a swim and a plate of ceviche that's literally fresh off the boat. A quiet little beach bar (no music) serves strong margaritas. Cabañas are for rent, but they're nearly buried in the sand.

El Paraiso Beach Club

Left on the coast road, 1.9km north of the junction ☎984/871-2007, ⊛www .elparaisotulum.com. The primary destination for sun-seekers who don't have beach access at their own hotels – particularly guests at the *Weary Traveler*, who get a free shuttle bus here every day – El Paraiso is a wide stretch of sand with plenty of palm trees and palapas for shade. The calm waters here are perfect for snorkelling – bring your own gear, or rent from the lively beach bar that dominates the scene (see p.143). If you want to escape the crowds, head north to the adjacent Playa Maya, a public beach with no services that's usually deserted.

Caleta Tankah Beach Club

2.8km north of Tulum ruins on Hwy-307 ⊛www.tankah.com.mx. $3. This mellow beach capitalizes on a pretty, protected cove, with palm trees for shade. A freshwater cenote lies at the mouth of the bay, making for a refreshingly cool temperature and a colourful mix of fish – rent snorkel gear from the bar to see them. The reasonably priced restaurant and a cluster of hammocks are the centre of the action (such as it is), but it's easy to wander away down the beach if you want to avoid the groups that come here for lunch as part of their package tours.

Gran Cenote

3.7km inland from Tulum on the road to Cobá. $5. Snorkellers will have a great time at this huge collapsed cavern with easy dock access and crystal-clear water. You can swim some 50m under the cavern ledges, and even into a second cenote entrance on the downstream side. The pool can get very busy in the middle of the day, as it's a popular stop for tours, but the dramatic rock formations are well worth braving crowds for. Also, because the water is partially covered by the rock overhang, summer algae growth on the water's surface isn't a problem.

Cenote Carwash (Aktun-Ha)

8km inland from Tulum on the road to Cobá. Swimmers and snorkellers $3, divers $5. From the surface, this cenote isn't as impressive as other popular swimming holes – it's simply a big pond, without any rock structure above – but strap on a snorkel mask or dive tanks, and you'll be astounded by the underwater rock formations, touted as among the best on the peninsula. Divers have an advantage here, as they can reach the spectacular Room of Tears cave, dripping with stalactites, and go below the algae bloom that thrives March through October, which makes snorkelling impossible.

Hidden Worlds

12km north of Tulum on Hwy-307
☎984/877-8535, ⊛www
.hiddenworlds.com.mx. Tours daily
9am–3pm. A cluster of outstanding cenotes and caverns are managed by a crew of cenote-diving experts. Guided group visits to the pools leave from the main entrance several times a day – choose from a one-hour snorkel tour of Hilario's Well ($25) or half-day snorkelling outings ($40–45) in the enormous underground cavern Tak Be Ha, the Bat Cave channel and the glimmering, sunlit Dos Ojos cenote – itself part of the second-longest underground cave system on the peninsula. The latter two also provide great opportunities for diving ($50 for one tank, $100 for two). Most impressive is the Dreamgate, an awe-inspiring 200-foot-wide cavern accessible only to divers. You can also visit some of these spots on your own, for a $5 entry fee paid at the Dos Ojos cenote, but if this is your first visit to a cenote, the tours add a great deal to the experience.

Casa Cenote

In Bahía Tankah, 8km north of Tulum; turn east from Hwy-307 on the road marked "Tankah Tres". This network of seven pools – some shallow, some fairly deep – winds through the trees and eventually feeds into the calm Bahía Tankah. There's no entrance fee, and you can have lunch at one of the two beachfront hotels there, Casa Cenote and Blue Sky. Bring your own snorkel gear, as it's not always available for rent from the hotels.

Xel-Há Ecopark

13km north of Tulum on Hwy-307.
☎984/875-6000, ⊛www.xelha
.com. Daily 9am–6pm. Mon–Fri $25,
kids $12.50; Sat–Sun $18, kids $9. All-inclusive $50, kids $25. A water park in the rough, this popular tourist attraction is built around a natural lagoon teeming with fish. The calm water, with numerous easy access points, is great for kids just getting used to snorkelling. You can float on inner tubes down the mangrove-lined river that feeds into the lagoon, or take the more adventurous snorkel tour through a small system of underground caverns. If the midday crowds get to be too much, a couple of secluded beaches provide respite. The entrance fee is steep (and doesn't include locker and snorkel rental), but if you have children and want to explore the natural features of the peninsula in a somewhat controlled environment, this is the place to go.

Across the road, the Xel-Há ruins (daily 8am–5pm; $3) are notable primarily for the extant stucco paintings in the Grupo Pájaros, on the east side of the site near the highway; miniature temples on the west edge resemble Tulum's, and a couple of cenotes dot the area.

Reserva de la Biósfera Sian Ka'an

Entrance and visitor centre on the coast road 9km south of the junction with the road to Tulum town. $2. Created by presidential decree in 1986, the nature reserve is one of the largest protected areas in Mexico, covering 1.6 million acres. The name means "the place where the sky is born" in Maya, which seems appropriate when you experience the sunrise on this stunningly beautiful coast. It's a huge, sparsely populated region, with only about a thousand permanent inhabitants, mainly

▲ RESERVA DE LA BIÓSFERA SIAN KA'AN

fishermen and subsistence farmers. Although you can enter the park unaccompanied, you will benefit more from an organized tour, which is easily arranged in Tulum (see pp.161–2).

Sian Ka'an contains the principal ecosystems found in the Yucatán peninsula and the Caribbean: approximately one-third of the area is tropical forest, one-third fresh- and saltwater marshes and mangroves, and one-third marine environment, including a section of the Mesoamerican Barrier Reef. The variety of flora and fauna is astonishing. All five species of Mexican wild cat – jaguar, puma, ocelot, margay and jaguarundi – live in the forest, along with spider and howler monkeys, tapir and deer. More than three hundred species of birds have been recorded, including fifteen types of heron and the endangered wood stork, the largest wading bird that breeds in North America. The Caribbean beaches provide nesting grounds for four endangered species of marine turtle, while some extremely rare West Indian manatees have

been seen offshore. Morelet's and mangrove crocodiles lurk in the swamps and lagoons. The coastal forests and wetlands are particularly important feeding and wintering areas for North American migratory birds.

Accommodation

Los Arrecifes

Right on the coast road, 3.1km south of the junction with the road to Tulum town ☎984/879-7307, ❾www .losarrecifestulum.com. Opened in the late Seventies on a particularly nice palm-studded beach, this is one of the oldest places on the coast, and it still provides a few basic one-bed, sand-floor wooden cabañas with shared bath ($20). More solid (if slightly sterile) cement-wall rooms with two beds (starting at $40) are also available, as is a "luxury cabana" with private bath for $100.

Azulik

On the coast road 800m south of the junction. ☎1-877/532-6737 for US reservations, ❾www.azulik.com. The most romantic option in the area: large wood cabins, all appointed with luxurious linens, are linked by a boardwalk through the trees. Deep tubs carved from tree trunks are set on the front terraces, which jut over the crashing surf, and a quiet beach lies just to the south. No kids allowed, and no electricity. Rooms from $185.

Boca Paila Camps

On the coast road, 10.8km south of the junction, inside the Sian Ka'an reserve ☎984/871-2499, ⊛www .cesiak.org. Sturdy tents are hidden among the trees at this rigorously ecological lodge built with minimal impact on the natural growth near the beach. All tents share bathrooms (with

composting toilets), but there is hot water, heated with solar and wind power. The staff, part of a non-profit environmental education group, is dedicated and informed, and the inexpensive restaurant is worth the long drive for its sunset view across the jungle. Doubles from $65, or dorm beds from $25 per person.

Cabañas Copal

On the coast road, 700m south of the junction. ☎1-877/532-6737 for US reservations, ⊛www.cabanascopal.com. The round, wood-floor cabañas are packed in pretty close here, but they feel roomy thanks to wall-size windows, making them a decent mid-range option

PLACES Tulum

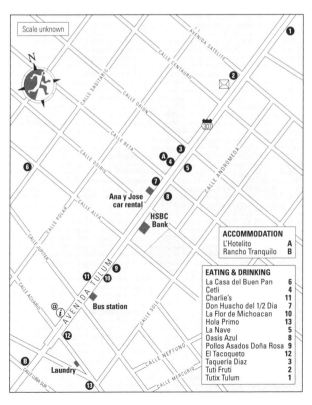

ACCOMMODATION	
L'Hotelito	A
Rancho Tranquilo	B

EATING & DRINKING	
La Casa del Buen Pan	6
Cetli	4
Charlie's	11
Don Huacho del 1/2 Dia	7
La Flor de Michoacan	10
Hola Primo	13
La Nave	5
Oasis Azul	8
Pollos Asados Doña Rosa	9
El Tacoqueto	12
Taquería Diaz	3
Tuti Fruti	2
Tutix Tulum	1

nonetheless. There's no electricity but plenty of hot water, and a clothing-optional beach. Services include bike rental and spa packages, including a *temazcal* – a New Age version of an ancient Mayan ritual sweat lodge. King beds from $60; two queen beds from $70.

Cabañas El Mirador
Left on the coast road, 2.6km north of the junction ☎998/845-7689, ⊛www.hotelstulum.com. Just south of where the coast road dead-ends against the ruins, this old backpackers' standby offers basic sand-floor cabañas with beds ($22) or hammocks ($15; bring your own or rent one of theirs). Shared bathroom with cold water. The on-site restaurant sits atop a cliff, with a wonderful view and cooling breezes.

▼CABAÑAS EL MIRADOR

Cabañas Zazil-Kin
On the coast road, 2.4km north of the junction ⊛www.hotelstulum.com /zazilkin.htm. Ownership change in 2004 (this was formerly the popular *Don Armando's*), the sturdy, sand-floor cabañas with shared baths were spruced up a bit. The place is still one of the most reliable of the inexpensive places near the ruins, with a buzzing restaurant-bar, a dive shop and good security – arrive as early in the day as possible. Doubles from $20.

El Crucero
East side of Hwy-307, at the first stoplight in Tulum town, by the pedestrian entrance to the archeological site ☎984/871-2610, ⊛www.el-crucero.com. Fun, friendly hotel convenient for visiting the ruins. Choose dorm beds ($7.50), standard rooms ($35) or deluxe rooms with a/c and distinctive murals painted by a local artist, who has a gallery on site. The bar-restaurant, with its outgoing American bartenders, is extremely hospitable and even has a wireless Internet hub.

L'Hotelito
Tulum town, west side of Av Tulum (Hwy-307) between C Orion and C Beta ☎984/871-2061, ✉hotelito@tulumabc .com. Guests are primarily Italian at this tiny hotel that has a country feel despite its location in the middle of town. The upstairs rooms have high palapa ceilings with fans ($40); downstairs rooms have a/c ($50). All look onto a small garden.

Nueva Vida de Ramiro
On the coast road, 4.5km south of the junction ☎984/877-8512, ⊛www .tulumnv.com. Peaceful, slightly quirky eco-hotel that relies entirely on wind turbines. The attractive wood cabins on stilts

▲EL CRUCERO

– all with front decks – as well as some newer cement cabins with exceptionally big tiled bathrooms, are carefully built over and around untamed greenery. The beach is splendid here, and the restaurant serves tasty seafood, big fruit shakes and great espresso. Doubles from $90.

Papaya Playa

On the coast road, 400m south of the junction ☎984/804-6444, ⊛www .papayaplaya.com. Good accommodation, with a bit of a party

scene, ranging from spacious cottages with private bath and hot water ($150, sleeping up to four) to clean, simple cabañas ($45 with two double beds). A small restaurant and bar, set on a cliff above the beach, plays chilled-out lounge beats. The adjacent *Tribal Village* (50m south from the junction), under the same ownership, has dorm beds for $12 per person.

El Paraiso

On the coast road, 1.9km north of the junction ☎984/871-2007, ⊛www .elparaisotulum.com. Set back a bit from the action at the beach club of the same name, this tidy, whimsically painted row of tile-floor rooms have porches and two double beds ($65). A few funkier oceanfront cabañas ($20) are also available – advisable only if you plan to join the party at the bar. No hot water.

La Posada del Sol

On the coast road, 1km south of the junction ☎984/876-6206, ⓔlaposadadelsol@hotmail.com. The four artfully designed, high-ceiling "jungle" rooms on the wooded side of the road are very large and an exceptional value; the three beachfront rooms cost a bit more, but are equally beautiful. Doubles from $65.

▼LA POSADA DEL SOL

Rancho Tranquilo

Tulum town, west side of Av Tulum (Hwy-307) two blocks south of the bus station ☎984/871-2092, ✉ranchotranquilo@hotmail.com. Basic bungalows in a garden full of fruit trees, starting at just $10 per person. For entertainment, go on a house-run fishing trip, or crack open a beer with the friendly owner.

Las Ranitas

On the coast road, 5.4km south of the junction ☎984/877-8554, ⊛www .lasranitas.com. This understated but comfortable French-owned hotel has fourteen well-designed breezy rooms and two family suites, tennis courts, a pool and an excellent library. Perhaps the biggest perk, however, is 24-hour electricity. Doubles from $170.

▼LAS RANITAS HOTEL

Sunscape Tulum

6km north of Tulum on Hwy-307 ☎984/871-3333, ⊛www .sunscaperesorts.com. A good-value, family-friendly resort that isn't dumbed down just to please kids. Four à la carte restaurants include a classy sushi bar, and the big rooms overlook hacienda-style courtyards. Children's activities are elaborate – overnight beach camping is one option. All-inclusive rack rates start at $195 per person; $50 for children.

Zamas

On the coast road, 1.2km south of the junction ☎984/871-2067, ⊛www .zamas.com. This long-established hotel popular with New Yorkers offers large thatch-roof rooms, some of which are enormous and right on one of the most scenic stretches of beach in the area. Hot water and electricity are plentiful, and the style is comfortably bohemian – minus the yoga. Good restaurant on site (see p.142). Doubles from $90.

Shops

Joyería Posada del Sol

On the coast road, 1km south of the junction with the road to Tulum town, in *La Posada del Sol*. The owners of this small hotel make delicate, nature-inspired jewellery and handicrafts. A few more typical souvenirs and postcards are available as well.

Mixik Artesanías

On the coast road, 1.2km south of the junction. Closed Sun. This dis-cerning gift shop stocks both Mexican kitsch, like colourful beer trays and papier-mâché Elvis skeletons, and quality crafts such as hand-blown glass and Oaxacan embroidery.

Cafés

Los Cántaros
East side of Hwy-307 at first stoplight in Tulum town, in front of *El Crucero hotel.* Tasty *nevería*, serving all flavours of sorbet, a refreshing treat after touring the ruins. Scoops, served in little handmade pitchers, start at $1.50.

La Casa del Buen Pan
Tulum town, C Sagitario Poniente at C Alfa. Savour the a/c along with a perfectly flaky croissant at this European-style bakery; there's also an adjacent garden for sipping organic coffee. Baking starts early – ring the bell if the door isn't yet unlocked.

La Flor de Michoacan
Tulum town, east side of Av Tulum (Hwy-307) between C Alfa and C Jupiter. Every town has one of these fresh-juice franchises, and Tulum's is especially welcome, painted bright pink and blasting cool air from its fridge cases. Go for straight juice or a refreshing *licuado* (fruit shake) or *agua de jamaica* (hibiscus).

La Nave
Tulum town, east side of Av Tulum (Hwy-307) between C Orion and C Beta. A busy town hangout with fresh-fruit breakfasts and inexpensive wood-oven pizza ($4.50 and up) and other Italian staples like fresh gnocchi ($6.50 and up).

Tuti Fruti
Tulum town, west side of Av Tulum (Hwy-307) between Av Satelite and C Centauro. Open 24hrs. The "Tortas Gigantes" sign is more prominent than the proper name on this small shack, and they're not kidding: massive sandwiches starting at $2, along with a full range of juices and *licuados*.

▲PASTRIES, LA CASA DEL BUEN PAN

Restaurants

Cetli
Tulum town, west side of Av Tulum (Hwy-307) between C Orion and C Beta, at L'Hotelito ☎984/745-9001. Closed Sun. Chef Claudia trained in Mexico City's premier culinary academy; at her tiny, casual restaurant in Tulum, she dishes up refined versions of Mexican classics, such as a delicate peanut-based *mole de cacahuete* ($7.50).

Don Huacho del 1/2 Dia
Tulum town, west side of Av Tulum (Hwy-307), between C Beta and C Osiris. The town's longtime Mexican seafood specialist (meat is relegated to the back page of the menu) features the mysteriously spiced *pescado a la Don Huacho* ($6), very fresh ceviche ($5) and tasty snacks like shark empanadas, great with beer.

Hechizo

On the coast road, 7.5km south of the junction, at *Rancho San Eric* (last driveway on the left before the Sian Ka'an entrance) ☎984/100-0170, ✉hechizo@bigfoot.com. Closed Mon and during fall. Chef Stefan (who trained with the *Ritz-Carlton* chain) and his wife Ying-Hui preside over this gem of a restaurant on the border of the nature reserve. The short, sophisticated international menu (watermelon-and-goat-cheese salad, lobster *pozole*) changes daily, accompanied by a solid wine list; appetizers are about $5, mains around $18. Call or email to reserve one of the eight tables.

Hola Primo

Tulum town, two blocks east of Av Tulum (Hwy-307) on C Acuario. This palapa-roof kitchen on the "Cancha Maya" (the plaza around the ceiba tree where the town was founded) caters to locals with *sopa de lima*, *panuchos* and *salbutes*. You can fill up on savoury snacks for less than $3.

Pollos Asados Doña Rosa

Tulum town, east side of Av Tulum (Hwy-307) between C Alfa and C Jupiter. Daily 11am–5pm. Basic but tasty roast chicken, Sinaloa-style (marinated in garlic and citrus juice), served on red-and-white-checked tablecloths for about $3 for half a chicken.

Posada Margherita

On the coast road, 2.5km south of the junction, at *Posada Margherita* hotel, ☎984/100-3780. Fantastic beachfront Italian restaurant with dishes like fresh taglierini with shrimp and zucchini and fish poached in sea water (both about $14). The antipasto platter, served on a slice of a tree trunk, is a bounty of piquant cheeses, cured meats and olives.

Qué Fresco

On the coast road, 1.2km south of the junction, at *Zamas*. Good Italian restaurant with a wood-fired pizza oven and fresh pasta, with mains from $8 to $18. Its beachside setting makes it great for breakfast, too – the Caribbean French toast ($4.50) is especially good.

El Tacoqueto

Tulum town, east side of Av Tulum (Hwy-307) at C Acuario. A dependable *lonchería* with gut-busting daily specials for $4 or delicious hot-off-the-grill tacos for even less.

Taquería Diaz

Tulum town, west side of Av Tulum (Hwy-307) between C Orion and C Beta. Closed Wed. Vying for the title of best *taquería* in town, at just

▼HOLA PRIMO

▲ LA VITA È BELLA

three for $2 – assorted grilled meat fillings are the speciality.

Bars

Charlie's
Tulum town, west side of Av Tulum (Hwy-307) between C Alfa and C Jupiter. Closed Mon. This long-running hangout with a Mexican menu (good guacamole) also hosts art shows and live music under its big palapa.

Oasis Azul
Tulum town, east side of Av Tulum (Hwy-307) between C Beta and C Osiris. Blue lights, a disco ball and a soundtrack of international techno and house hits set the party tone at this hip bar. Sit out front on the sidewalk and sip a drink, or pack onto the small dance floor in the back.

El Paraiso Beach Club
On the coast road, 1.9km north of the junction. This very hospitable beach bar has plenty of room for dancing on the sand. A big screen shows movies, or trippy visuals during the occasional massive parties.

La Vita è Bella
On the coast road, 1.6km north of the junction. A young European crowd frequents this giant sand-floor palapa equipped with big speakers and Ibiza beats; the cocktail bar opens at 9.30pm, but dancing doesn't start until after the kitchen (reasonably priced sandwiches and wood-oven pizzas, as well as grilled meats) closes at 11pm. No cover, unless it's a few dollars for a big organized party – usually around the full moon.

The inland ruins

Travelling from the Caribbean coast to the quiet rural interior provides a fine change of pace from the beach scene. The dense forest here, dotted with archeological sites and tiny villages, is essential for anyone intrigued by the region's Maya heritage. Three hours from Cancún, the ruined city of **Chichén Itzá** is a vast, legendary complex dominated by towering El Castillo, one of the great icons of Maya culture. Largely bypassed by those en route to Chichén Itzá, the site of **Ek-Balam** bears rare and perfectly intact stucco decoration, and has only been open to the public for a few years. A bit more than an hour's drive southeast from Chichén Itzá sprawls **Cobá**, an older city that has been only partially dug out of the jungle. While all of these sites can be visited on day-trips from Cancún, the centrally located colonial city of **Valladolid**, with its gracious plazas, old churches and affordable hotels, makes an excellent base for exploring the area.

Valladolid

Around 40km east of Chichén Itzá, the small city of Valladolid is still close enough to beat the crowds to the site on an early bus, and of interest in its own right. Although it took a severe bashing in the nineteenth-century Caste Wars, when Mexican armies clashed with the local Maya resisting central-ized rule, the town has retained a strong colonial feel and centres on a pretty, peaceful *zócalo*, or main plaza – at its finest at dusk, when the curving love seats are filled with chatting couples, and the bubbling fountain of a woman in a traditional Yucatecan *huipil* dress is lit.

Valladolid is defined by its scenic colonial churches – the

Visiting the inland ruins

Express buses run inland from Cancún to Valladolid ($9; 2hr) several times a day and to Chichén Itzá ($12; 2.5hr) at 9am. To make your way back, an express bus to Cancún leaves Chichén Itzá at 4.30pm. From Tulum, four buses a day run via Cobá ($2.80; 30min) to Valladolid ($5.10; 1.5hr); two continue to Chichén Itzá ($7.80; 2hr). From Valladolid, express buses run hourly to Chichén Itzá ($2; 40min) starting at 7.15am, but $1.50 **colectivos** (from Calle 44 just off the plaza) are cheaper and run more frequently. Ek-Balam is not yet served by buses; take a *colectivo* from Calle 44 in Valladolid. **Driving** inland from Cancún on Hwy-180, the fast toll highway (*cuota*) is preferable to the free road (*libre*) if you're going all the way to Chichén Itzá ($18).

The **tourist office** in Valladolid is on the southeast corner of the plaza, on Calle 40 at Calle 41 (Mon–Sat 9am–8.30pm, Sun 9am–1pm), though it's often left unattended.

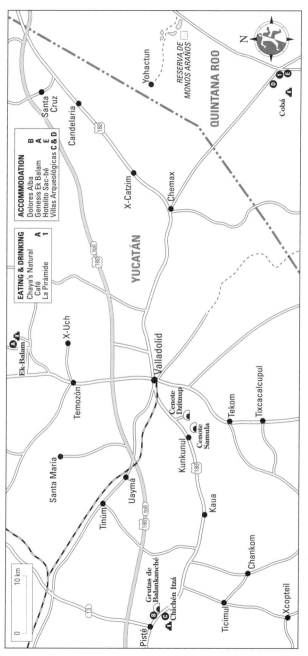

PLACES

The inland ruins

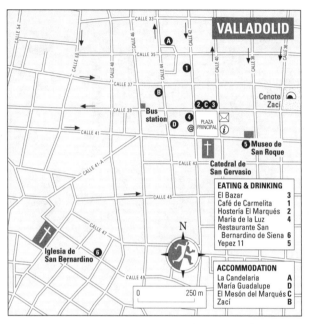

VALLADOLID

EATING & DRINKING

El Bazar	3
Café de Carmelita	1
Hostería El Marqués	2
María de la Luz	4
Restaurante San Bernardino de Siena	6
Yepez 11	5

ACCOMMODATION

La Candelaria	A
María Guadalupe	D
El Mesón del Marqués	C
Zací	B

▼COLONIAL CHURCH, VALLADOLID

twin white towers of one, the Catedral de San Gervasio, loom over the south side of the plaza. The oldest church is the sixteenth-century Iglesia de San Bernardino de Siena, 1km southwest of the *zócalo* (daily except Tues 9am–8pm; Mass daily at 6pm). Built over a cenote, the church buildings are massive, but there's little left inside as they were sacked by the local Indians during the Caste Wars; only a fine Baroque altarpiece remains.

East of the *zócalo* on Calle 41 is a smaller historic church, now converted to the Museo de San Roque (Mon–Sat 9am–9pm; $2). Objects from the site of Ek-Balam, craftwork from nearby villages and contemporary Maya altars to the rain god Chac comprise the museum's small but diverse collection. Valladolid's other tourist attraction is Cenote Zací, on the block formed by calles 34, 36 and 37 and 39 (daily 8am–6pm; $1). Right in the middle of the city, it's probably the easiest cenote to visit, with broad stairs leading down into a huge cavern where light reflects off the green water and glimmers on the walls. The air is cool and refreshing, and an open-air restaurant affords a fine view and excellent photo opportunities. Swimming is possible, but unlike at many cenotes, it is not encouraged – there are no changing facilities.

Chichén Itzá

Daily 8am–6pm. $8. The most famous, most extensively restored and most visited of all Maya sites, Chichén Itzá is nearly synonymous with its great pyramid, **El Castillo** (also called the Pyramid of Kukul-cán), a simple square building with a monumental stairway ascending each face, rising to a temple at the top. The building is the Maya calendar rendered in stone: each staircase has 91 steps,

▲EL CARACOL OBSERVATORY, CHICHÉN ITZÁ

which, added to the single step at the entrance to the temple, amounts to 365. Near sunset on the spring and autumn equi-noxes, the serpents' heads at the foot of the main staircase are

The rise and fall of the ancient Maya

Though Maya civilization dates back as far as 2600 BC, it was not until about 250 AD that this extraordinary culture begin to flourish, with the city of **Tikal** in Guatemala ushering in the **Early Classic period**. Over the next several centuries, Maya influence spread as far as the Yucatán in the north to Honduras in the south. Wealth grew from a strong network of urban centres, linked through trade and strategic alliances. Perhaps the finest example of these thriving cities was majestic **Palenque**, in what is now Chiapas, which was most densely populated around 700, during the **Late Classic period**.

By the beginning of the **Post-Classic period** around 900, however, Palenque and other major population centres were all but abandoned. It appears that the rapid collapse was triggered by an environment that simply could not support so many people – a severe drought between 800 and 1050 exacerbated an existing food and resource shortage, leading to political instability and the end of centralized power.

In the wake of this catastrophe, however, the Yucatán cities blossomed, with **Chichén Itzá** becoming the first power of the Post-Classic era. Eventually, though, the Itzá clan too waned, and the peninsula splintered into independent city-states. Only a few coastal cities continued long-distance trade and were still at it when the Spanish arrived in the sixteenth century. After this point, many Maya were enslaved and the last of their cities were reclaimed by the jungle.

The inland ruins

CHICHÉN ITZÁ

N

180

Cenote Sagrado

CHICHÉN NUEVO

Sacbé

Pisté & Mérida

Templo Norte

Gran Juego de Pelota

Parking

Tzompantli

Plataforma de Venus

Plataforma de Aguilas y Jaguares

Templo de los Jaguares

Templo de los Guerreros

Visitors Centre & Main Entrance

El Castillo

Grupo de las Mil Columnas

Juego de Pelota

El Osario

Plataforma de las Tumbas

Juego de Pelota

Casa de los Metates

Temazcalli

Templo del Venado

Mercado

Casa Colorada

Cenote Xtoloc

East Entrance

Hotel Mayaland

El Caracol

CHICHÉN VIEJO

Templo de los Tableros

Akab-Dzib

Edificio de las Monjas

La Iglesia

Annexe

Villas Arqueológicas

0   100 m

Highway to Valladolid & Cancún

Exploring Chichén Itzá

A huge **visitor centre** occupies the western entrance to the ruins; here you can arrange group tours in one of four languages (Spanish, English, German or Italian) for up to twenty people (approx $30) or private tours for a little more, though most people tour the site on their own. At the smaller, eastern entrance in front of *Hotel Mayaland*, you can book two-hour horseback tours around Chichén Viejo ($48 with guide).

The nightly **sound-and-light** show (7pm in winter, 8pm in summer; $3, or included in price of day entrance ticket), on the plaza in front of El Castillo, is a bit of a yawn, though it does re-create the shadow-serpent effect on the Castillo. It's worth seeing only if you're staying nearby.

joined to their tails at the top by an undulating body of shadow.

Inside El Castillo an earlier pyramid survives. An entrance (11am–3pm, 4–5pm) at ground level connects to a narrow stair leading up to a temple on top, which contains one of the site's greatest finds: a jaguar altar painted bright red and inset with jade spots and eyes.

The **Templo de los Guerreros** (Temple of the Warriors) and the adjoining Grupo de las Mil Columnas (Group of the Thousand Columns) form the eastern edge of the plaza in front of El Castillo. The columns are warriors in armour, their arms raised above their heads, while the temple is decorated with Toltec-style eagles devouring human hearts as well as with Maya masks of the rain god Chac, with his distinctive curling nose. West across the plaza is the **Águilas y Jaguares** platform, adorned with more eagles tearing hearts from victims. It was likely the site of human sacrifices, judging by the proximity of the gruesome Tzompantli platform, where victims' skulls were displayed.

The **Juego de Pelota**, on the western side of the plaza, is the largest known ball-court – some 90m long. The target rings are halfway along each side, and sloping panels depict scenes of the game and its players, shown processing towards a central

▼LOOKING DOWN GRUPO DE LAS MIL COLUMNAS, CHICHÉN ITZÁ

PLACES The inland ruins

The Toltec debate

Though the ruins of Chichén Itzá have come to symbolize the Maya, the city's divergence from Maya tradition is what makes it so archeologically intriguing. Experts are fairly certain that the city rose to power between 800 and 1000 AD, but the rest of its history, as well as the roots of the ruling Itzá clan, remain hotly disputed.

The emphasis on human sacrifice, the presence of a huge ball-court and the glorification of military activity all point to a strong influence of the **Toltec culture** in central Mexico. For decades researchers guessed this was the result of the city's defeat by the Toltecs, a theory reinforced by the resemblance of the Templo de los Guerreros to the colonnade at Tula, near Mexico City, along with numerous depictions of the Toltec god-king, the feathered serpent Quetzalcoatl (Kukulcán to the Maya).

Recent work, however, supports the theory that the Itzá people were not Toltec invaders, but fellow Maya who had migrated from the south (an explanation for their subjects referring to them as "foreigners" in texts). The Toltec artefacts, this view holds, arrived in central Yucatán via the Itzá's chief trading partners, the Chontal Maya, who maintained allegiances with Toltecs of Central Mexico and Oaxaca.

circle, the symbol of death. One player, just to the right of the centre, has been decapitated, while another (to the left) holds his head and a ritual knife. On the outer east wall of the court, the **Templo de los Jaguares** is a little portico supported by two pillars with a stone jaguar between. Inside, the elaborate relief carvings show the Itzá ancestors inserted in the Maya creation myth – a powerful demonstration of their entitlement to rule.

The **Cenote Sagrado** lies 300m down the *sacbé,* or causeway, that leads off the north side of the plaza. It was regarded as a portal to the "other world", called Xibalba. The Maya threw offerings into it – incense, statues, jade and especially metal disks engraved with figures and glyphs – as well as human victims.

South of El Castillo lies **Chichén Viejo** ("Old Chichén"), where the buildings are not so well restored. Remarkable, however, is El Osario, a miniature version

of El Castillo; El Caracol, which resembles a modern-day observatory and has slits in its roof that correspond with various astronomical points; and the so-called Monjas (nunnery) building, its eastern annexe finished in an elaborate monster-mouth mask of Chac.

Grutas de Balankanché

On Hwy-180 libre 4km east of Chichén Itzá. Tours daily at 11am, 1pm & 3pm. $5. Second-class bus from Valladolid or Chichén Itzá, or *colectivo* from C 44 in Valladolid ($4). In 1959 a sealed passageway was discovered here leading to a series of caverns in which the ancient population had left offerings to the god Chac. Guided tours – in reality, a taped commentary – lead you past the stalactites and stalagmites, an underground pool and, most interesting, many of the original Maya offerings. Be warned that in places the caves can be cold, damp and thoroughly claustrophobic. When the caves were discovered, a local traditional priest insisted on carrying out an exorcism ritual to placate the ancient gods and disturbed spirits.

Cenotes Dzitnup and Samula

5km west of Valladolid on Hwy-180 libre, then 2km south at a signposted turn. The remarkable Cenote Dzitnup, also called X'Keken (daily 7am–6pm; $2), is reached by descending into a chilly cave where a nearly circular pool of crystal-clear turquoise water is illuminated by a shaft of light from an opening in the roof – a sight that transfixes photographers and swimmers. Across the road is the equally impressive Cenote Samula (daily 8am–5pm; $2), where the roots of a huge tree stretch down into a pool. While Dzitnup is frequently crowded with people on bus tours and plagued by small children asking for tips, you may well find yourself alone at Samula.

Colectivos ($1.50) run to Dzitnup from outside the *Hotel María Guadalupe* in Valladolid (p.154). You can also cycle from Valladolid on a paved bike path. In town, rent bikes from the Rey de Béisbol sports shop, Calle 44 between calles 39 and 41.

Ek-Balam

15km north of Valladolid. Daily 8am–5pm. $2.40. Little visited but well excavated, Ek-Balam is notable for the high quality and unique details of its sculpture. The city, enclosed by a series of defensive walls, was occupied from the Preclassic period, perhaps as early as 500 BC, through the Spanish conquest.

Enter through a freestanding four-sided arch; beyond are two identical temples, called **Las Gemelas** (the Twins), followed by a long ball-court. The principal building is the massive structure called **La Acropolis**, the base of which was built in 600 BC.

Thatched awnings protect elaborate stucco work only discovered in 1994 – 85 percent of what you see is original, unretouched plaster from the ninth century.

Just below the summit is a doorway in the form of a giant gaping mouth, studded with protruding teeth. It is the entrance to the **tomb** of Ukit-Kan-Lek-Tok, the city's powerful king in the mid-ninth century. The lower jaw forms the floor; the skulls, lilies, fish

PLACES The inland ruins

▼EK-BALAM

and other symbols of the underworld carved below reinforce its function as a tomb gateway. Of the detailed human figures that surround the door, one's disproportionate limbs and deformed hands and feet suggest it is a portrait of a real person; one theory has it that this deformation was a result of inbreeding in the royal class. The figure at the top centre of the mouth is thought to be the king himself.

Back on the ground, in the plaza, an exceptionally well-preserved **stela** depicts a king receiving the objects of power from Ukit-Kan-Lek-Tok, the smaller figure at the top of the stela, seated with one leg folded under.

Given the rich detail at the site, which takes about an hour to see properly, it's worth hiring a guide for about $25 for a small group. Juan Canul, who has worked on many excavations, is recommended; ask for him at the ticket desk.

Cobá

55km southeast of Valladolid; 50km northwest of Tulum. Daily 7am–6pm. $3.70. The crumbling ancient city of Cobá is a fascinating site, as much for the wildlife as for the ruins. The jungle here is home to toucans, egrets, coatis and myriad tropical butterflies. You'll need at least a couple of hours to see everything; inside, you can rent bikes for $2.50, or hire a *triciclo* cab for $7.50, or $10 with a guide.

Occupied from about 100 AD until the arrival of the Spanish, the city's zenith was in the Late Classic period, around 800 AD, when most of the larger pyramids were built and its wealth grew from close links with the great cities of Petén, in lowland Mexico and Guatemala, which also influenced the architecture and the use of stelae, usually seen only in the southern Maya regions.

The first cluster of buildings is the compact **Grupo Cobá**, with a large central pyramid known as the Iglesia (church), used for Maya ceremonies even after the city had ceased to function. Claustrophobic corbel-vault passages lead a little way inside. Up the main path, at a fork, the **Grupo de Pinturas** was built with recycled stones in the Late Post-Classic, after 1200, when the city saw a surge of new building. Along the left path is a small ball-court, only one side of which has been excavated – the stone skull carving set in the ground is a marker found in most courts. Just behind the ball-court is the **Xaibé** (Crossroads) pyramid, so named for its position at a major junction of *sacbeob*, the lime-paved highways the Maya built to connect cities; the pyramid's rounded, stepped design is typical lowlands building style.

The path ends at the looming **Nohoch Muul**, taller than El Castillo at Chichén Itzá and resembling in its narrow and precipitous stairway the pyramid at Tikal in Guatemala. At the top is a small temple, similar to structures at Tulum, dating from 1200. The view takes in nearby lakes, as well as the jungle stretching uninterrupted to the horizons.

Back at the central fork, another path leads 1km to **Grupo Macanxoc**, a cluster of some twenty stelae, most carved during the seventh century AD. Stela 1 shows part of the Maya creation myth and the oldest Long Count date on record – more than 41 thousand, million, million, million, million years

▲ COBÁ

prior, according to the highly complex Mayan calendar. Other stelae depict an atypically high number of women, suggesting that Cobá may have had female rulers. Clambering between the carvings, you're crossing not natural hills, but unreconstructed pyramids.

Reserva de Monos Araños

18km northeast from the Cobá roundabout or 22km southwest off Hwy-180 libre at Nuevo X-Can. $3 per person, plus $15 for a guide for a group of up to ten people. This reserve at the small village of Punta Laguna was created for scientific observation of one of the northernmost populations of nimble, playful spider monkeys. From the small entrance kiosk, you are required to hike with a guide to where the animals usually congregate – there's no guarantee you'll see them, but they're at their liveliest in the early morning and the late afternoon. The trail winds past unrestored ruins and a cenote, and in the middle of the reserve is a big brackish lake where you can rent canoes ($5) and paddle around looking for herons and crocodiles.

To reach the area you'll need a car, though some Cobá tours from Tulum (inquire at your hotel) and Valladolid (through *La Candelaria* hostel) include a visit to the reserve. Pack food, snacks and snorkel gear for the cenote, as there are as yet no concessions nearby.

Accommodation

La Candelaria

C 35 between C 44 and C 42, Valladolid ☎ 985/856-2267, ✉ candelaria_hostel@hotmail.com. This excellent hostel next to one of Valladolid's many churches has clean dorm rooms and a pretty garden. It also offers Internet access, bike rental and tours to the surrounding natural and archeological attractions. Dorm beds from $8.

Dolores Alba

Hwy-180 libre Km 122, 2km east of Chichén Itzá ☎ 999/928-5650, ✇ www .doloresalba.com. The best-value hotel near Chichén Itzá, with clean, colourful rooms, a good restaurant and two swimming pools, one of which was created out of a natural spring. The staff are very helpful and provide transport to the site (but not back). Doubles from $33.

Genesis Ek Balam

Village of Ek-Balam, 2km west of the ruins ☏985/858-9375, ⓦwww.genesisretreat.com. This impeccably designed eco-retreat boasts a garden filled with flowering plants, beautiful outdoor showers and a bio-filtered pool. All rooms (one with a/c) have shared baths. The hospitable Canadian owner, who built the place herself, can arrange tours and activities with the local Maya in the tiny village. Rates from $15 per person.

Hotel María Guadalupe

C 44 no. 198, between C 39 and C 41, Valladolid ☏985/856-2068. This is the best of the cheapies in Valladolid, with clean, well-kept rooms with baths and a/c in a small, vaguely groovy two-storey building. *Colectivos* for Cenote Dzitnup leave from outside. Doubles from $17.

Hotelito Sac-bé

On the west side of the main road in the village of Cobá ☏984/879-9340. A relatively new offering in Cobá (and vastly superior to the only other budget choice, a dingy place up the street): five clean rooms with a choice of hot ($20) or cold ($15) water, and even a/c ($30). Inquire at the very informal post office across from the bus stop if no one's at the hotel.

El Mesón del Marqués

C 39 no. 203, on the *zócalo*, Valladolid ☏985/856-2073, ⓦwww .mesondelmarques.com. This lovely hotel is set in a former colonial mansion. The courtyard contains fountains, lush plants, a palm-fringed pool, and a great restaurant (see opposite). Doubles from $50, including full breakfast.

Villas Arqueológicas

Near the east entrance to Chichén Itzá ☏985/858-1527, ⓦwww.clubmed .com. This Club Med-operated hotel provides a bit of affordable luxury, complete with a swimming pool and an archeological library. It's not as posh as its neighbours on the east road into the ruins, but far better value. Doubles from $62. Another *Villas Arqueológicas*, with the same rates, overlooks the lake at Cobá.

Zací

C 44 no. 191, between C 39 and C 37, Valladolid ☏985/856-2167. Pleasant modern three-storey hotel with a quiet courtyard; the big rooms have either a fan or, for a few dollars more, a/c and cable TV. A small pool makes it a great bargain. Doubles from $25.

Cafés

Café de Carmelita

C 42 no. 183, between C 35 and C 37, Valladolid. An inexpensive spot serving granola breakfasts and salads to backpackers from the nearby hostel, as well as more typical local fare like *enchiladas de mole*. Classic Mexican ballads on the stereo set a cosy, nostalgic tone.

Chaya's Natural Restaurant

At the *Genesis Ek Balam* retreat, 2km west of the Ek-Balam site. A great place to stop after visiting the ruins – treats include avocado ice cream, chocolate-chile cookies and, of course, all sorts of dishes featuring the healthy and savoury spinach-like *chaya* plant.

Restaurants

El Bazar

Northeastern corner of the *zócalo*,
C 39 at C 40, Valladolid. A dizzying selection of inexpensive
loncherías and pizzerias, always
busy and open late – about the
only place in town aside from
Hostería El Marqués to eat after
9pm.

Hostería El Marqués

C 39 no. 203, on the *zócalo* in *Mesón
del Marqués*, Valladolid. Valladolid's
best restaurant is set in a tranquil
interior courtyard. Yucatecan
dishes such as the classic chicken
soup, *sopa de lima*, and orange-
marinated *poc-chuc* pork are
on the menu, along with great
examples city specialities like
lomitos de Valladolid (spicy stewed
pork loin) and *escabeche de Valladolid* (chicken in a sweet-sour
broth). Prices are reasonable,
starting at $6 for mains.

María de la Luz

C 42 on the *zócalo*, Valladolid.
Popular terrace restaurant with
a basic Mexican and Yucatecan
menu, including local dishes like
the bright-red *longaniza* pork
sausage. Good-value breakfast
buffet ($4.50).

La Pirámide

At the end of the road leading to the
Cobá ruins. Set beside the lake
between the ruins and the village,
this is a solid choice for an
affordable lunch of Yucatecan specialities as well as other Mexican
dishes – all priced around $7.

Restaurante San Bernardino de Siena

C 49 no. 227, two blocks behind
Convento San Bernardino, Valladolid.
Locally known as *Don Juanito's*
and frequented mostly by Mexicans, this highly recommended,
mid-price restaurant is a great
family-run place for a lazy
lunch or dinner away from the
hustle and bustle of the town
centre. Grilled fish and meat are
the specialities.

Bars

Yepez II

C 41 opposite Museo de San Roque,
Valladolid. Daily till 2am. Friendly
semi-open-air bar and restaurant
with live music after 9.30pm,
as well as very cheap Mexican
snacks (tacos from $.50, *queso
fundido* for $2). Families come
for dinner, but the crowd
becomes predominantly male
(not too rowdy though) once
the music starts.

Essentials

Arrival

Most visitors to **Cancún** will arrive at the city's international airport (@ www .cancun-airport.com), 20km south of downtown Cancún and just inland from the lower end of the *zona hotelera*. In each of the airport's two terminals, ATMs are located just outside customs. Buses and shuttle vans run to downtown Cancún and to every hotel on the beach – a 20- to 45-minute ride, depending on where you're headed.

It's also possible to fly directly to **Cozumel**; the airport is on the north edge of San Miguel. If you arrive in Cozumel via the ferry from Playa del Carmen, you are deposited directly in front of the town square, where it's easy to flag a cab to your hotel. The cruise-ship piers are just south of San Miguel, with Punta Langosta being the closest, on the southern edge of town; the International pier and Puerta Maya are about 4km from downtown.

Information

Online resources provide an easy way to prepare for your trip, with a variety of sites containing useful information on Cancún and Mexico's Caribbean coast. The Riviera Maya Tourism Board (@ www .rivieramaya.com) and the Mexico tourist board (@ www.visitmexico.com) have good basic intros to the Caribbean coast. Check out tips and forums at Playa del Carmen Info (@ www .playadelcarmeninfo.com), Cozumel Insider (@ www.cozumelinsider.com) and Cozumel My Cozumel (@ www .cozumelmycozumel.com). For details on the Sian Ka'an Biosphere Reserve, see the sites maintained by Amigos de Sian Ka'an (@ www.amigosdesiankaan .org) and the Centro Ecológico Sian Ka'an (@ www.cesiak.org). The official Valladolid site (@ www.chichen.com.mx/valladolid) is a good introduction to the town and surrounding sights.

Also look into excellent maps from @ www.cancunmap.com, which can give you a detailed lay of the land before you go – especially useful if you're considering renting a private house or condo and want to know it's precise location and what's nearby.

Once in Mexico, local tourist offices are usually a good place to start, though none are equipped to make hotel reservations. Playa del Carmen's *La Quinta* magazine, which details the town's trendier side, is available for free in many bars and restaurants. The *Miami Herald Cancún Edition*, an English newspaper, will give you insight into local political issues, and the excellent monthly flyer *Entérate Cancún*, available in some bookshops and coffee houses downtown as well as online (@ www.enteratecancun.com), details the arts scene. Note that kiosks offering "tourist information" are usually not officially sanctioned – they're pushing timeshares.

Transport and tours

If you'll be spending most of your time in **Cancún**, you'll find it's easy enough to get around by bus and taxi. On **Cozumel**, you can walk or ride a bike around town, but a car is necessary to explore the southern and eastern portions of the island, as there is no bus service. **Playa del Carmen** and **Isla Mujeres** are both small enough for walking or riding a bicycle to be the best option. In Tulum, it's handy to have a car for a visit there, to get between the beach area and the main town and to visit nearby cenotes, but you can also count on taxis. To see the inland ruins or visit several towns along the coast, buses provide regular service but a car affords more flexibility and saves time.

Buses

Buses in **Cancún** run every couple of minutes through the *zona hotelera* along Paseo Kukulcán and into the downtown area. Many also run along Avenida Tulum and up to the Ultramar ferry dock for Isla Mujeres. The fare is $0.65 to and within the hotel zone and $0.45 within downtown. There are several route numbers, but all are clearly marked "Hoteles".

Bus service along the **Caribbean coast** from Cancún is frequent, inexpensive and comfortable. For most intercity routes, you can check **schedules** and buy **tickets** online at ⊛ www.ticketbus .com.mx. Mayab and Riviera offer the most frequent services, on comfortable buses; ADO is the primary long-distance first-class carrier. Traveling inland, Valladolid and Chichén Itzá are well served by ADO, but with nowhere near the frequency of the coastal buses.

On Isla Mujeres, two bus lines run from Avenida Medina in the main town down to the southern end of the island for just $0.30, but you'll have more flexibility and fun with a bike, moped or golf cart.

Taxis

Within towns, **taxis** can be a quick, relatively affordable way to get around: In Cancún, they're plentiful and can be hailed almost anywhere – the trip between downtown and Punta Cancún in the *zona hotelera* costs around $9. Prices will be higher in cars hired at restaurants and hotels (where prices should be posted). Always tell your driver your destination and agree to a fare before getting in. Be on guard against drivers who will insist that the hotel you've requested has closed, in an attempt to reroute you to a place that will pay them a commission; reports of this practice are high in Tulum.

Shared taxis – large sedans or passenger vans called *colectivos* or *combis* – provide a more flexible way of travelling between towns, especially in the interior or to the cenotes along Hwy-307 north of Tulum. The vehicles meet at fixed points in each town and depart whenever they're full. You can also flag them down anywhere along the highway, and they'll stop if they have a vacant seat. Pay the driver when you get off. *Colectivos* from Valladolid to Chichén Itzá leave from Calle 44, and cost just $1.50; the same goes for Ek-Balam.

If you're travelling with a few other people, a regular taxi can be economical for an out-of-town ride – a ride from Tulum to the ruins of Cobá costs about $21, for example. Hotels can arrange for cars, or you can negotiate directly with a driver at a taxi rank, which will probably result in a better price.

Cars

A **car** is a boon for travellers with a limited amount of time. The roads in this part of Mexico are good, save for the rutted southern stretch of the Tulum hotel zone. Mopeds are advised against, as traffic on Hwy-307 is very heavy, and there's always a risk of a sudden downpour.

Local **car rental agencies** quote prices that include all taxes and insurance (typically about $50 per day), but be sure to check the terms before you sign. International agencies such as Hertz require drivers to be at least 25 years old, but many locally owned companies will rent to 21-year-olds. If you book with an international company, online discounts are substantial and reservations can often be made up to a few hours in advance.

A few **road rules** can make driving simpler. Most important, if you wish to make a left turn, pull into the farthest *right* lane, or the shoulder if possible, then put on your left-turn signal and turn only when all lanes are clear. A driver who wants to pass will flash his headlights; you're expected to pull to the right and slow a bit to hasten the process. Rural roads (including the free highway to Chichén Itzá) are punctuated by large, sometimes unmarked **speed bumps** (*topes*). If not crossed at an absolute crawl, they can do serious damage to your car's under-carriage. At any sign of population, slow down and be alert.

Car rental agencies

Cancún Buster Rent a Car, Blvd Kukulcán Km 3.5 (☎998/849-7221, ☎849-4394, ☎www.busterrentacar.com); Europcar, Av Nader 27 (☎998/884-4714).
Playa del Carmen Localiza, Av Juárez between Av 5 and Av 10 (☎984/873-0580).
San Miguel (Cozumel) Rentadora Isleña, C 7 between Av Melgar and Av 5 (☎987/872-0788, ☎www.cozumelhomes.com).
Tulum Ana y José, Av Tulum (Hwy-307) between C Beta and C Osiris (☎984/871-2030, ☎www.anayjose.com).

Bicycles and golf carts

Getting around by **bike** is practical only on Isla Mujeres, in Playa del Carmen and the town of San Miguel on Cozumel. A bike can also be pleasant in Valladolid, where a dedicated bike path runs out of town to nearby cenotes. Prices range from $8 to $15 per day, depending on

the town. Be sure to check all the brakes and gears before you set out.

Golf carts are a popular mode of transport on Isla Mujeres. You can make a complete tour of the island on a single charge, and rates are typically about $15 per hour.

Ferries

Isla Mujeres is served by ferries from Cancún; for Cozumel, ferries depart frequently from the piers in central Playa del Carmen. See the relevant chapters for times and prices. Car ferries also run to both islands, but they are erratic, expensive and slow – you're better off renting a car on Cozumel, or a bike or golf cart on Isla Mujeres.

Tours

Organized tours can provide educated and unique perspectives on plants, animals and local culture. For inland ruins, a multi-site tour can be useful if you're pressed for time – but if you can't find an itinerary that matches your needs exactly, you might be better off renting a car.

Tour operators

AeroSaab ☎984 873-0804, ☎www.aerosaab.com. The most efficient – and expensive – way to visit Chichén Itzá is by private plane: flights on four- or five-passenger Cessnas from Playa del Carmen or Cozumel from $270 per person, including a tour guide and a cenote swim.
Alas at *Posada Freud* on Av 5, Playa del Carmen ☎984/871-4020. Twenty-minute rides above Playa in an ultralight plane for $80.
Alltournative C 38 between Av 1 and Av 5, Playa del Carmen ☎984/873-2036, ☎www.alltournative.com. A major operator of ecologically minded group tours of various kinds, usually involving some active sport and a visit to a local community. Headquarters are in Playa del Carmen, but they will pick up from most hotels on the coast. Half-day tours from $68; full-day, $90.
Atlantis Carretera Costera Sur Km 4, Cozumel ☎987/872-5671, ☎www.atlantisadventures.com. A real submarine

dives to 100 feet in Parque Chankanaab – pricey at $79 ($45 for kids) for a 40-minute tour, but a great way to see the reef life.
Goyo's Jungle Tours Av Rojo Gómez one block north of the plaza, Puerto Morelos ☎998/871-0189, ✆www.mayajungle.com. Small tours to inland cenotes, from $40; also runs a *temazcal* (sweat lodge) for just $25 per person.
Jungle Buggy Tours C 7 between Av Melgar and Av 5, San Miguel ☎987/872-0788, ✆www.cozumelhomes.com. Full-day tours in a fleet of dune buggies up the northeast coast of Cozumel, with lunch and time to snorkel ($90).
Maya Echo Puerto Morelos ☎998/871-0136, ✆www.mayaecho.com. Sandra Day-

ton is active in the local Maya community – many of her tours involve visits to nearby villages and education on culture and spirituality. She also leads sweat lodges, tours of the botanical gardens on Hwy-307, and trips to traditional markets in Cancún.
Sian Ka'an Info Tours Hwy-307 in front of *El Crucero* hotel, Tulum ☎984/871-2499, ✆www.siankaan.org. Runs a day trip ($65) and a sunset tour (only in bird migration season, Nov–April; $40) inside the nature reserve. Both begin with an instructive walk through mangroves and diverse ecosystems to a large cenote, followed by a boat ride across the lagoons and the ancient Mayan canals that crisscross the marshy areas here.

Costs and money

Compared to other parts of Mexico, Cancún and the Caribbean coast has a reputation for being expensive. Indeed, in Cancún a hotel room on the beach can rarely be had for less than $100 per night, and prices in restaurants are comparable to those in big American cities. Cozumel is only marginally cheaper, as the tourist infrastructure caters to divers willing to spend quite a lot. However, both places can be visited on a budget, as can the intervening beach towns, which offer a broader range of facilities. Bargain hunters in Cancún should head to the downtown area, particularly for meals; the town of San Miguel is less expensive away from the blocks immediately surrounding the ferry dock, and if you're diving, a package deal of accommodation and boat trips can save money.

The currency of Mexico is the new *peso*, designated by "$" or "M$". *Pesos* are divided into one hundred *centavos*, but you will rarely see anything smaller than a 50 *centavo* coin. Many tourist-oriented services post prices in US dollars, written as "US$1", "$1 Dll" or "USD 1". The exchange rate is typically around ten *pesos* to one dollar, but if you are uncertain, clarify ("Pesos o dólares?") before paying. Many businesses in Cancún will take US dollars in payment, or give them in change.

You'll get the best exchange rate by withdrawing cash from an ATM (*caja permanente* or *caja automático*), provided your home bank does not charge substantial fees for using your card outside the country. **ATMs and banks** are plentiful in Cancún, Cozumel and Playa del Carmen; Tulum, Isla Mujeres and Valladolid have a few, and Puerto Morelos has an ATM but no bank. Money-changing agencies (*casas de cambio*) are a last resort. Travellers' cheques are easily changed, and credit cards widely accepted, though generally only cash is used at less expensive hotels and restaurants. **Bank hours** are usually Mon–Fri 9.30am–3pm, Sat 9.30am–1pm; HSBC banks stay open until 7pm on weekdays.

A note about prices

Due to the fluctuation of the *peso*, prices are quoted in this guide in US dollars.

Accommodation

Accommodation options along the Caribbean coast range from rustic sand-floor cabañas lit by candles to luxurious pleasure palaces in which all your meals and drinks are prearranged. Travellers looking for smaller hotels have plenty of choice, whether friendly guesthouses on remote beaches, unhosted apartment rentals or stylish and comfortable hotels in the middle of the action in Playa del Carmen. In Cancún's *zona hotelera*, however, "small" generally means fewer than three hundred rooms; with a few exceptions, the more intimate hotels are all in the downtown area. One agent representing a number of smaller, well-designed resorts, hotels and apartments is the US-based Turquoise Reef (☎ in the US on 1-800-538-6802, ✆ www .mexicoholiday.com).

All-inclusives

All-inclusive resorts are the most popular lodging choices, and the package deals they offer can be enticing even to travellers who ordinarily wouldn't consider them. For parents travelling with younger children, all-inclusives are free of fuss and provide a programme of activities to keep kids occupied. If you're considering this option, though, don't skimp – cheaper places may seem like a bargain on paper, but the facilities can be run-down and the meals bor-

dering on inedible. Plus, prepaid meals may be a waste if you're enticed into the many excellent restaurants in Playa del Carmen, for instance. Many resorts in Cancún that were built as all-inclusives are now becoming more flexible, offering the option of breakfast only or no meals at all (also called a European plan).

Ecoresorts

A growing trend on Mexico's Caribbean coast is to stay in a so-called **ecoresort**. "Eco-" is a freely used prefix, and often hotels will tout their use of solar panels and wind turbines not because they've chosen this option but because they simply don't have access to the electric grid – as is the case on the beach in Tulum. A truly environmentally sound hotel will also have a wastewater treatment system, a composting procedure and a building plan that minimizes impact on plant and animal life – as well as, ideally, an economic and social relationship with the surrounding native culture. *Boca Paila Camps* in the Sian Ka'an reserve (p.137) is an excellent example, as is *Genesis Ek Balam* near the ruins north of Valladolid (p.154). Note that it's not necessarily less expensive to run a hotel without steady power or running water – go "eco" because you support the premise, not for a bargain.

Accommodation prices

All hotel rooms are subject to a 12 percent **tax**. Some hotels – generally those under $40 per night – build this into the quoted rate, while most others add it to the bill. Prices listed in this guide don't include tax, and are typically based on the cheapest double room in **high season** (Jan–April). Playa del Carmen and Tulum have a second high season in July and August, when Europeans take their vacations. Everywhere sees an additional price hike for the week between Christmas and New Year and the week before Easter, a major Mexican holiday period. At smaller hotels, it's worth asking for a discount if you walk in off the street; for larger, chain-owned resorts and hotels, booking ahead is the only way to negotiate something lower than the official rack rate.

Food and drink ESSENTIALS

Food and drink

The food of the **Yucatán peninsula** is fresh and varied – a mix of earthy local specialities that have been cooked in some form since the pre-Columbian era alongside dishes from other regions of Mexico, brought by people who've moved to this area in the last few decades. You can also choose from an array of international flavours, from sushi in Cancún to delicate handmade pasta and imported prosciutto in the Italian-influenced areas of Playa del Carmen and Tulum.

In the coastal towns, you'll of course enjoy a great deal of wonderfully fresh **fish**, shrimp, rock lobster and conch, which you can order simply grilled, fried with garlic or made into ceviche – doused in lime and left to "cook" in the acidic juice with tomato, onion and plenty of coriander.

You'll find more typical **Yucatecan specialities** inland; many dishes contain juice from bitter oranges and *achiote* (also called *adobo*), a mellow spice that lends a characteristic orange glow to food. Little of it is hot – that's the job of the incendiary red or green *salsa de habañero* set on most tables.

Vegetarians will have some trouble, as meat is ofen added as flavouring even to vegetable side dishes. But quesadillas, with tasty and nutritious toppings such as cactus leaves and squash blossoms are easy to find.

At **breakfast**, many people eat tacos, but there's also no shortage of *pan dulce* (pastry), fresh fruit, granolas and yoghurt, as well as honey and bee pollen – the Maya have been keeping bees for centuries. Good coffee is grown in neighbouring Chiapas, but it's usually brewed weak and often flavoured with cinnamon. **Lunch** is the big meal of the day, served from noon until 3pm or so. The best (and some of the least expensive) local restaurants are open only for lunch, so plan accordingly if sampling local delicacies is a priority. Budget restaurants usually offer a daily special, called the

comida corrida or *comida corriente*, that for about $4 gives you a large entrée as well as various extras such as beans and a drink. **Dinner** is traditionally tacos, tortas and the Yucatecan *panucho*, a sort of *tostada*, often served in casual palapas or from kiosks and carts. Resorts of course serve a more lavish buffet or dinner in an à la carte restaurant, and all of the beach towns also have European-influenced restaurants that serve full meals from 6pm to 10pm.

Drink

A wide selection of **nonalcoholic drinks** are available, although the saturation of Coca-Cola advertisements might make you think otherwise. A popular juice blend is pineapple and spinach-like *chaya* – sweet and healthy-tasting. Fruit and ice-cream stands offer refreshing *licuadas* (fruit puréed with a little water or milk) and a big selection of *aguas*, light, water-based beverages.

Margaritas are the de facto **beach drink**, and the standard **beers** are the light pilsners Sol and Superior and the slightly darker Dos Equis and the Yucatán-brewed Montejo. Look also for fuller-bodied (and more expensive) beers like Bohemia and Negra Modelo. A popular beer treatment is the *michelada*, in which beer is seasoned with lime, hot sauce and Worcestershire sauce and served in a salt-rimmed glass with ice; a *chelada* is just the lime, ice and salt. When ordering, say what type of beer you'd like it made with: a *michelada de Sol*, for example. *Xtabentun*, a sweet, herb-infused liqueur (anise predominates), has its roots in ancient Maya techniques. Mexico's **wine** production is improving, and some, from Baja California and some other northern states, are quite good – look for them in better restaurants such as *Yaxche* (p.111) and *La Habichuela* (p.76).

A note on **water**: in Cancún, it is thoroughly treated and safe to drink, if not very tasty. Elsewhere, stick to bottled water, but generally you needn't be too wary of ice or juices, because Mexicans themselves are accustomed to using purified water for everything. More important to health is general hygiene (wash your hands frequently) and proper hydration (go easy on the margaritas).

Sports and outdoor activities

Cancún and the Caribbean coast are paradise for the active traveller, with diving, snorkelling, kiteboarding and more within easy reach.

Diving and snorkelling

With the vibrant and complex **Meso-american Barrier Reef** running directly offshore, this part of Mexico's coastline, particularly around Cozumel, is one of the top scuba-diving destinations in the world. Snorkellers can also enjoy some of these undersea wonders – in spots, it's possible to wade to the reef from shore, while a boat trip (with an experi-enced guide) can make a visit to a more remote coral garden or wall an easy and rewarding experience. With so many dive spots – and countless dive shops willing to take you there – it's important to choose an outfit wisely and be clear and honest about your diving skills and experience. A respectable divemaster should not push you to a more advanced dive; it helps if you can find a group of divers of roughly the same level and approach a shop together. Some old hands dive only with guides who have families, a good indicator that your leaders won't be taking unnecessary risks at your – or their – expense. On Cozumel, would-be snorkellers will want an operator who's willing

Exploring coral reefs

Coral reefs are among the richest and most complex ecosystems on earth, but they are also very fragile. The colonies grow at a rate of only around 5cm per year, so they must be treated with care and respect if they are not to be damaged beyond repair. Remember to follow these **simple rules** while you are snorkelling, diving or in a boat.

Never touch or stand on corals, as the living polyps on their surface are easily damaged.

Avoid disturbing the sand around corals. Apart from spoiling visibility, the cloud of sand will settle over the corals and smother them.

Don't remove shells, sponges or other creatures from the reef, and avoid buying reef products from souvenir shops.

Don't use suntan lotion in reef areas, as the oils are pollutants and will stifle coral growth; look for special biodegradable sunscreen for use while snorkelling.

Don't anchor boats on the reef: use the permanently secured buoys instead.

Don't throw litter overboard.

Check ahead of time where you are allowed to go fishing.

If you are an out-of-practice diver, make sure you **review** your diving skills away from the reef first.

to travel the distance to the best spots on Colombia and Palancar reefs.

The best coral growth and fish life is around Cozumel, and parts of that are accessible from Playa del Carmen as well. The reef off Puerto Morelos is relatively untouched. Cancún is not known for diving, though some spots are excellent for novices, with sandy floors, little current, easy access and plenty to see. Isla Mujeres has easily accessible snorkelling off the Sac Bajo Peninsula as well as a couple of interesting wreck dives.

The Yucatán also offers the unique experience of diving in the freshwater sinkholes called **cenotes**, part of the vast network of underground rivers, caves and caverns that riddle the granite bedrock that forms the peninsula. The pristine spring water is gin-clear, and the elaborate rock formations otherworldly. Although many dive shops offer cenote diving packages, not all have the experience to back it up, and most of the tragic cave-diving accidents have been the fault of guides who took the sport too lightly. Nonetheless, cavern diving (in which you explore a partially open space, with the entrance in clear view) requires only open-water certification; to go deeper into passageways and closed caves, you'll need excellent buoyancy control. **Snorkelling** can be enjoyed by anyone at a number of cenotes – where the owners often rent gear as well. An underwater flashlight can be a big help.

Dive shops

Almost Heaven Adventures, north side of the plaza ☎998 871-0230, ⓦwww .almostheavenadventures.com. Certification courses and one- and two-tank dives ($40–55), as well as sport-fishing charters (approx $225 for up to four people; 5–6hr) and snorkelling trips ($22 per person; 2hr).
Blue Angel, in the *Caribe Blu* hotel south of San Miguel ☎987-872-1631, ⓦwww .blueangel-scuba.com. Also recommended, especially for classes.
Cancún Manta Divers, Playa Tortugas, Blvd Kukulcán Km 6.5 ☎998/849-4050, ⓦwww.mantadivers.com. Operating more than a decade; small-group trips in Cancún or to Cozumel and various cenotes.

Cozumel Deep Blue, Av Salas at Av 10 ☎987/872-5653, ⓦwww.deepbluecozumel .com. Very professional and knowledgeable; two-tank dives for $65.
Isla Mujeres Coral, C Matamoros 13-A ☎998/877-0763, ⓦwww .coralscubadivecenter.com. Trips to the Cuevas de los Tiburones Dormidos and to El Frío wreck dive; two-tank dives for $59.
Playa del Carmen Tank-Ha, Av 5 between C 8 and C 10 ☎984/873-0302, ⓦwww .tankha.com. Runs PADI and SSI certification courses ($275) and one- and two-tank dives ($40–60) as well as twice-daily snorkelling tours (9am & 1.30pm; $30; 3hr). Sealife Divers, at *Mamita's* in North Beach ☎984/803-2866, ⓦwww. sealifedivers.com. Experienced in cave diving ($100 for a two-tank dive).
Puerto Morelos Dive Puerto Morelos, Av Rojo Gómez north of the plaza ☎998/206-9084, ⓦwww.divepuertomorelos.com. Trips to the local reef, as well to inland cenotes and Cozumel.
Tulum Aktún Dive Center, Hwy-307 at the beach road ☎984/871-2311, ⓦwww .aktundive.com.Cenote diving specialist, with specialized cave diving courses ($300–1100) as well as cavern snorkelling tours ($30).

Windsurfing and kiteboarding

Windsurfing conditions are decent in Cancún – the trick is finding areas that aren't too crowded. Escuela de Tabla Vela (Blvd Kukulcán Km 3, ☎998/842-9072) is conveniently located on the flat, calm bay water, away from hotels, so students have room to maneuver. A two-hour introductory course is $45. On the east coast of Cozumel, *Mezcalito's* rents boards.

More recently, the sport of **kiteboarding** has taken hold on the emptier beaches around Puerto Morelos and Tulum. The main school is Ikarus, with headquarters in Playa del Carmen on Avenida 5 between Constituyentes and Calle 16 (☎984/803-2068 ⓦwww .ikaruskiteboarding.com); classes start at $60 per hour. In Cancún, Koko Dog'z, Av Nader 42-A (☎998/887-3635), is another expert in all extreme water sports; there's a second shop in Puerto Morelos, north of the plaza near the *Ojo de Agua* hotel.

Other water activities

Both **jet skiing** ($50 for 30min) and **parasailing** ($40 for 10min) are very popular in Cancún; operators are dotted at frequent intervals in front of the big hotels on the beach. Aquaworld (Blvd Kukulcán Km 15.2, ☎ 998/848-8327, ◍ www.aquaworld.com.mx), is the main purveyor of water fun, offering **"jungle" tours** (ride two-person speedboats through the lagoon mangroves, then out to Punta Nizuc to snorkel), diving excursions and outings to Isla Mujeres. There's also the unique *SubSee Explorer*, a glass-bottom boat ($35 for a 45min trip) in which passengers are seated well below the waterline – no bending over to see the sea life. **Sailing** is another option, particularly on the calm bay between Cancún and Isla Mujeres; rent your own catamaran at Escuela de Tabla Vela ($30 per hour). If you'd rather leave it to the experts, Two Much Fun 'n a Boat, at the Blue Bay dock, Blvd Kukulcán Km 3.5 (☎998/105-5667, ◍www.twomuchfun-n-aboat.com), runs four-hour sailing excursions to Isla Mujeres ($40) with time out for snorkeling.

Sport-fishing is excellent all along the coast. In Cancún, *Villas Manglar* hotel specializes in fishing packages; in Puerto Morelos, the dive shop Almost Heaven Adventures also organizes fishing excursions; in Tulum, contact Victor Barrera for trips inside the Sian Ka'an reserve (☎ 984/879-8040, ◍ www.macabimarch.com).

Golf

The Caribbean coast's temperate climate and diverse terrain have inspired several excellent golf courses. Greens fees range from $100 to $150.

Golf courses

Club de Golf Cancún Blvd Kukulcán Km 7.5 t998/883-1230, wwww.cancungolfclub.com. The 18 holes (72-par total) provides sweeping views of both the lagoon and the sea.

Cozumel Country Club Carretera Costera Norte Km 6.5 ☎987/872-9570, ◍www.cozumelcountryclub.com.mx. This Jack Nicklaus-designed par-72 course is built around a large lake; some of the 18 holes are set in patches of jungle and mangrove.

Cozumel Mini-Golf C 1 at Av 15 ☎987/872-6570, ◍www.cozumelminigolf.com. Mon–Sat 10am–11pm, Sun 5–11pm $7, kids $5. A suitably tropical 18-hole course complete with waterfalls and ponds, with a couple of added benefits: you can select the music you'd like to hear played on the course, and you can order drinks by walkie-talkie.

Hilton Cancun Golf Club Blvd Kukulcán Km 17 ☎998/881-8000, ◍www.hiltoncancun.com. This course on the lagoon side makes creative use of the setting, with a mangrove trap, a tee on an island and a view of the El Rey ruins from the 18th hole.

Playacar Golf Club Carretera Cancún-Tulum Km 72 ☎984/873-0624, ◍www.palace-resorts.com. The most challenging play in the area, dotted with ruins and cenotes. Fees are all-inclusive: a drinks cart makes the rounds of all 27 holes (the last nine, added in 2004, have a dune setting).

Yoga

Classes are given at hotels up and down the coast, but particularly on the beach in Tulum. The *Maya Tulum* resort is the oldest dedicated yoga retreat in the area, and offers twice-daily classes, usually in the hatha style, to non-guests for about $10 (on the coast road, 2km south of the junction with the road to Tulum town, ◍www.mayatulum.com).

Festivals and events

January 6

Epiphany Presents are traditionally given on this night, when the three Magi of the Bible arrived bearing gifts, rather than on Christmas. Though not a public holiday, many stores and businesses close up shop.

February–March

Carnaval The week before Lent is celebrated with fervour on Cozumel, with parades and eye-popping costumes and wild masks. Isla Mujeres also has a sizeable celebration.

Mid-March–June

Baseball season The major-league Cancún Langosteros play at Estadio Beto Ávila (p.71). Every other town has one or two baseball fields where you can while away a summer night – the atmosphere is casual, and entrance fees are nominal.

Mid-March–mid-April

Spring break Cancún is the destination for hordes of college-age American students – either a draw or a deterrent, depending on your perspective.
Vernal equinox (March 21) Thousands of visitors flock to Chichén Itzá to witness the moment when the serpent heads on the main staircase of El Castillo are joined to their tails by a fantastic play of light and shadow. It's preceded by some loose ritual that's simultaneously spiritual and schlocky.
Semana Santa Mexico's biggest holiday is Holy Week, beginning on Palm Sunday and continuing until Easter Sunday. Still a deeply religious festival in Mexico, it celebrates the resurrection of Christ, and has also become an occasion to venerate the Virgin Mary, with processions bearing her image a hallmark of the celebrations. During Semana Santa, expect transport to be totally disrupted, as everyone is on the move. Many places close for the whole of Holy Week, and certainly from Thursday to Sunday.

Late April–early May

Fiesta de la Santa Cruz The village of El Cedral on Cozumel hosts this two-week festival commemorating the arrival of the conquistadors on the island and the first Catholic mass in the Western hemisphere on May 6, 1518.

Mid-May

Regatta al Sol Isla Mujeres is the finish line for this biannual yacht race (even-number years) that begins in Pensacola, Florida. When the boats arrive, the island throws a big parade and party.

Late May

Cancún Jazz Festival The city plays host to headline acts from around the world, tinged with a Latin flavour. Venues are throughout the *zona hotelera* and in some small clubs downtown.

Last weekend in May

Torneo de Pesca Deportiva Puerto Morelos has hosted this annual sport-fishing tournament since 1989. To participate, you have to supply a boat and crew; otherwise, just show up for the Saturday-night dance in the town square.

June 26–30

Fiesta de San Pedro y San Pablo A big party in San Miguel, Cozumel, with fair rides, food stalls and dancing.

September 16

Día de la Independencia This national holiday marks the historic moment in 1810 when the Catholic priest Manuel Hidalgo y Costilla called for liberation from the tyranny of the Spaniards from his parish church in Dolores Hidalgo. It's now marked at midnight on September 15 with a mass recitation of the *grito* – the impassioned cry of "Mexicanos, viva México!" – in every town's main square, followed by fireworks, music and dancing. In Cancún, the greater part of the month is given over to festivities.

September 21

Autumnal equinox This day marks another serpent spectacle at Chichén Itzá,

Public holidays

Jan 1 New Year's Day

Feb 5 Anniversary of the Constitution

March 21 Benito Juárez Day

Good Friday and Easter Saturday

May 1 Labour Day

May 5 Battle of Puebla

Sept 1 Presidential address to the nation

Sept 16 Día de la Independencia

Oct 12 Día de la Raza/Columbus Day

Nov 1 & 2 All Saints Day/Day of the Dead

Nov 20 Anniversary of the Revolution

Dec 12 Día de la Virgin de Guadalupe

Dec 24–26 Christmas

though it's not quite as heavily attended as the spring festivities.

September 29
Celebración de San Miguel Another fair takes over the main plaza on Cozumel, this time commemorating the town's patron saint.

November 1 & 2
Día de los Muertos All Saints and All Souls' Day and its eve is when offerings are made to ancestors' souls, with picnics and all-night vigils at their graves. People build shrines in their homes to honour their departed relatives, but it's the cemeteries to head for if you want to see the really spectacular stuff. Sweetmeats and papier-mâché statues of dressed-up skeletons lend the proceedings a macabre yet cheerful air.

November 1–17
Cancún International Gastronomic Festival A celebration of food and wine, with high-end hotel chefs from all over the world showing off their skills in special dinners and events in the *zona hotelera*.

December 12
Día de la Virgen de Guadalupe On Isla Mujeres, this national celebation is particularly special, as it commemorates one of three miraculous statues of the Virgin Mary discovered in Boca Iglesia in 1890. One was brought to Isla Mujeres, and over time a host of legends has built up around it. The festival lasts for the first week in December, ending in the rededication of the church on the main plaza.

December 25
Christmas A major holiday, and again a time when people are on the move and transport is booked solid. Gringo influence is heavy nowadays, with Santa Claus and Christmas trees, but the Mexican festival remains distinct in many ways, with a much stronger religious element (virtually every home has a nativity crib).

December 31
New Year's Eve This night is still largely an occasion to spend with family, the actual hour celebrated with the eating of grapes.

Shopping

Shopping for good quality items on Mexico's Caribbean coast can be difficult, given the glut of cheap T-shirts and knick-knacks that clutter most store shelves. But a few local specialities make unusual gifts and keepsakes. In particular, silver **jewellery** (genuine sterling should be stamped ".925"), often set with colourful

semiprecious stones, rich amber or milky Mexican opals, can be elegant and inexpensive. In duty-free Cozumel, shops specialize in gemstones – but it's wiser to window-shop unless you're an expert, as quality is not always as high as touted. Cotton clothing is often well made and cut in modern styles – or look for traditional

huipiles, the delicately embroidered white smocks that Yucatecan women wear. Quality and price can vary substantially, but Valladolid is a good place to shop because many of the surrounding towns specialize in embroidery. Other good buys include Panama **hats** (known here as *jipis*) and local crafts like elaborately painted gourds and masks and marvellous papier-mâché figurines.

The most popular local souvenir is a **hammock**. If you want something you can realistically sleep in, never buy from street vendors or even a market stall – goods are invariably of very poor craftmanship. Comfort is measured by the tightness of the weave and the breadth: because you're supposed to lie in a hammock diagonally, to be relatively flat, the distance it stretches sideways is far more crucial than the length (although obviously the woven portion of the hammock, excluding the strings at each end, should be at least as long as you are tall). A good way to judge quality is by weight: a decent-size hammock (*doble* at least, preferably *matrimonial*) with cotton threads (*hilos de algodon*, more comfortable and less likely to go out of shape than artificial fibres) will weigh more than a kilo and set you back about $25. ("Sisal" hammocks are generally fraudulent; this rough rope material is seldom used today.)

In Cancún and Playa del Carmen, you'll have plenty of opportunity to buy Cuban **cigars** and a dizzying array of **tequila** (even the selection in the supermarkets can be quite good). *Reposados* are somewhat aged tequilas that have taken on a faint woody taste from their casks – much more complex than your standard José Cuervo. *Añejos* are aged longer; some approach whiskey or scotch in their smoky complexity.

Bargaining and haggling are very much a matter of personal style, highly dependent on your command of Spanish, aggressiveness and experience. The old tricks (never show the least sign of interest, let alone enthusiasm; walking away will always cut the price dramatically) hold true; but most important is to know what you want, its approximate value and how much you are prepared to pay. Never start negotiating for something you don't intend to buy. In shops you have little chance of significantly altering the official price unless you're buying in bulk, and even in markets most food and simple household goods have a set price. In any case, the best price is the one both you and the seller are happy with.

Directory

Airlines Aerocaribe/Aerocozumel, Plaza América Av Cobá 5 ☎998/884-2000; Aeroméxico ☎800/021-4000 or Av Coba 80 ☎998/884-1097 or at the airport ☎886-0018 or in Cozumel ☎987/872-3454; American ☎800/904-6000 or at the *Fiesta Americana Coral Beach* ☎998/883-4461 or at the airport ☎886-0129; Aviacsa, ☎800/006-2200 or Av Cobá 37 ☎998/887-4211 or at the airport ☎998/886-0093; Continental ☎800/900-5000 or at Cancún airport ☎998/886-0006 or at Cozumel airport ☎987/872-0847; Delta ☎800/123-4710, or at the airport ☎998/886-0668; Iberia ☎998/886-0158 or in Cozumel, Av Melgar 17, ☎987/872-3456; Magnicharters, Av Nader 93 ☎998/884-0600; Mexicana ☎800/502-2000 or Av Tulum 269 ☎998/881-9090 or at *Dreams Cancun* ☎848-7091 or in Cozumel at Av Melgar 17 ☎987/872-2945; Northwest/KLM ☎800/900-0800 or at the airport ☎998/886-0044; United ☎800/003-0777; US Airways ☎800-007-8800.

Airport enquiries Cancún ☎998/848-7220; Cozumel ☎987/872-0485.

American Express In Cancún, Av Tulum 208, at C Agua (Mon–Fri 9am–5pm, ☎998/884-4000).

Beaches Nominally all beaches in Mexico are public, but those tended by mega-resorts will make non-guests feel unwelcome. Beach clubs, while not the deserted beach of fantasy, often provide great service and amenities for a small minimum in food or drink. Be careful when swimming at unattended beaches – the open Caribbean can be quite rough, with strong currents and undertows. Nude sunbathing is illegal (except at a few specialized resorts), but going topless is fairly common, particularly in Playa del Carmen and Tulum.

Bowling Kukulcán Bol in Cancún (Plaza Kukulcán, Blvd Kukulcán Km 13 ☏998/885-3425; daily 10am–1am) is a great way to pass a rainy day. It's popular with locals, too, and hosts league nights – call ahead in the evenings to make sure some lanes are free.

Cinemas Cancún: Cinépolis and Cinépolis VIP (with leather chairs and waitress service) at Plaza Las Américas, Av Tulum ☏www.cinepolis.com.mx, and Cinemark in La Isla Shopping Village, Blvd Kukulcán Km 12; Cozumel: Cinépolis at Av Melgar 1001 between C 15 and C 17; Playa del Carmen: Cines Hollywood in Plaza Pelicanos, Av 10 at C 10.

Consulates Canada: Plaza Caracol, Blvd Kukulcán Km 8.5 ☏998/883-3360; Germany: Punta Conoco 36 ☏998/884-1898; Netherlands: Martinair office at the airport ☏998/886-0134; UK: at the *Royal Sands*, Blvd Kukulcán Km 13.5 ☏998/881-0100; US: Plaza Caracol in Cancún ☏998/883-0272, Plaza Villamar in Cozumel ☏987/872-4574, ☏www .usembassy.org.mx.

Disabled travellers This part of Mexico is not very accommodating to travellers with limited mobility, with steep sidewalks and non-accessible buses. One fine exception is *Posada Margherita* in Tulum (p.142), a small, fully wheelchair-accessible resort with a divemaster trained in working with disabled divers. Otherwise, it's safest to stick to Cancún (where more hotels have ramps and elevators), and to travel in taxis.

Electricity Current is the same as in the US and Canada, 110 volts at 60Hz; plugs are the same, too, with two flat slots.

Emergencies General emergency ☏080; police ☏060; fire ☏068; ambulance ☏065; Green Angels (emergency highway breakdown) ☏555/250-8221; toll-free tourist advice ☏800/903-9200.

Gay and lesbian travellers Cancún, which hosts an international gay festival every May, has a small scene (mostly male) at the *Karamba* club (p.77) and *Picante*, a bar on Avenida Tulum north of Avenida Uxmal (☏www.picantebar.com). There's some discreet cruising at Playa Delfines on the weekends. In Playa del Carmen, *Club 69*, on Avenida 5, is the main gay nightclub; *Bloo*, on Calle 6 between avenidas 20 and 25, is a smaller bar with a lesbian night on Wednesdays and a Sunday afternoon dance party.

Internet Internet cafés are ubiquitous and, except for in the Cancún's *zona hotelera*, cheap – between $1 and $2 per hour. Some that offer exceptional service are the Crew Office in Cozumel (Av 5 between Av Salas and C 3 Sur), which can also transfer images from your digital camera to a CD, and Cosmic Cosas (C Matamoros at Av Hidalgo) in Isla Mujeres, which has a cable for laptop hookups. Wireless hotspots are still very rare, though Tulum's hostel and info center, *The Weary Traveler*, has one.

Left luggage Upstairs in Cancún's bus station is a luggage-storage facility, where you can drop bags ($0.40 to $1 per hour). At the airport, there are luggage lockers past customs in the main terminal.

Mail and post offices Mail delivery times are erratic. Airmail postcards and letters under 20g cost $0.85 to the US and Canada, $1.05 to Europe and $1.15 to Australasia. Main post offices in Cancún: Av Sunyaxchén at Av Xel-Ha (Mon–Fri 8am–6pm, Sat 9am–1pm); Cozumel: Av Melgar at C 7 Sur (Mon–Fri 9am–4pm, Sat 9am–1pm); Isla Mujeres: C Guerrero at C Mateos (Mon–Thurs 9am–4pm); Playa del Carmen: Av Juárez between Av 15 and Av 20 (Mon–Fri 8am–4pm); Tulum: Av Tulum (Hwy-307) between C Satelite and C Centauro (Mon–Fri 9am–4pm).

Opening hours Only the smallest towns still take any kind of siesta, and businesses are generally open from 9am to 5 or 6pm, and are closed one day a week – usually Monday, but this can vary by town.

Pharmacies A *farmacia* should be your first stop for basic medical advice, as pharmacists are well informed and accustomed to diagnosing as well as prescribing. Additionally, a wide range of inexpensive generic prescription drugs are available without a prescription, and pharmacies in Playa del Carmen and Cancún cater specially to this trade.

Spas Spas and saunas are a major part of some resorts – and some are open to non-guests. *Temazcal* saunas (Maya-style sweat lodges) are popular, and involve varying degrees of spiritual guidance. In Cancún, the spa at *Le Meridien* is excellent and not prohibitively expensive; in Playa del Carmen, *Itzá Spa* on Calle Corazón (☎984/803-2588, ✆www.itzaspa.com) has open-air showers, a rooftop sauna and a varied menu of massages and treatments.

Telephones The least expensive option is a public pay phone, operated by Ladatel or Telmex – you must have a corresponding phone card purchased from a stationer. It's easier to stop into a *caseta*, or phone office, which may have off-peak special rates and is always cheaper than calling from your hotel. When dialing within a town, use the seven-digit number; for calls to another town, dial 01 followed by the three-digit area code and the number. For international calls, dial 00 followed by the country code, area code and number. Mobile phone networks are the same as the US: predominantly TDMA, with some 850/1900Mhz GSM coverage (which is not exactly the same as European GSM systems) in Cancún.

Time Same as the Central time zone in the United States, GMT –6, or GMT –5 during summer time (first Sunday in April till last Sunday in October).

Tipping In restaurants, generally tip ten percent, though fifteen percent is often expected in Cancún. Service (*servicio*) is sometimes included in the bill, in which case you are not required to leave more. Cab drivers need to be tipped only for dealing with baggage; gas station attendants should receive \$0.50 to \$1 for washing windows or checking oil. Restroom attendants should receive \$0.30 to \$0.50. For housekeeping in hotels, tip in keeping with international standards: \$1 or \$2 per day per guest. Tour guides also expect tips.

Travel agents Most hotels above the budget level have an on-site agency to book rental cars, arrange tours and work with airlines. Otherwise, the student-friendly agency Nómadas is a good bet in Cancún, at Av Cobá 5 (☎998/892-2320, ✆www .nomadastravel.com).

Visas and passports Visiting Americans and Canadians are technically required to present only a government-issued ID, along with a birth certificate – but a passport is far more convenient. Visas are not required for citizens of the US, Canada, the EU countries, Australia and New Zealand; other nationalities should inquire at the local Mexican embassy. All visitors are issued a tourist card that can be valid for 180 days, but immigration officers normally write in 15 or 30 – if you need longer, be sure to request it, as the process of getting an extension requires a tedious visit to an immigration office and a fee of \$20.

Language

Spanish

Once you get into it, Spanish is a straightforward language – and in Mexico people are desperately eager to understand and to help the most faltering attempt to speak it. English is widely spoken, especially in the tourist areas such as Cancún and Playa del Carmen, but you'll get a far better reception if you at least try to communicate with people in their own tongue. You'll be further helped by the fact that Mexicans speak relatively slowly (compared with Spaniards) and that there's none of the awkward lisping pronunciation.

Pronunciation

The rules of pronunciation are fairly clear cut and strictly observed.

A   is between the A sound of "back" and that of "father"
E   as in "get"
I   as in "police"
O   as in "hot"
U   as in "rule"
C   is spoken like S before E and I, hard otherwise: *cerca* is pronounced "serka".
G   is a guttural H sound (like the ch in "loch"); before E or I, a hard G elsewhere: *gigante* becomes "higante".
H   is always silent.
J   the same sound as a guttural G: *jamón* is pronounced "hamon".
LL sounds like an English Y: *tortilla* is pronounced "torteeya".
Ñ   with the tilde (accent), spoken like NY: *mañana* sounds like "manyana".
QU is pronounced like an English K.
R   is rolled, RR doubly so.
V   sounds more like B, *vino* becoming "beano".
X   has an S sound before consonants; between vowels in place names, it has an H sound, like México ("meh-hee-ko"). In Maya words, X sounds like SH – so Xel-Ha is pronounced "shel-ha".
Z   is the same as a soft C, so *cerveza* becomes "servesa".

Useful terms and phrases

Basics		With, Without	Con, Sin
		What?, How much?	¿Qué?, ¿Cuánto?
Yes, No	Sí, No	Good, Bad	Buen(o)/a, Mal(o)/a
Open, Closed	Abierto/a, Cerrado/a	Here, There	Aquí/Acá, Allí/Allá
Please, Thank you	Por favor, Gracias	Big, Small	Gran(de), Pequeño/a
Push, Pull	Empujar, Tirar	This, That	Este, Eso
Where?, When?	¿Dónde?, ¿Cuándo?	More, Less	Más, Menos

LANGAUGE

Useful terms and phrases

Today, Tomorrow	Hoy, Mañana
Cheap, Expensive	Barato/a, Caro/a
Yesterday	Ayer
Now, Later	Ahora, Más tarde

Greetings and responses

Hello, Goodbye	¡Hola!, Adiós
Good morning	Buenos días
Good afternoon/ night	Buenas tardes/ noches
How do you do?	¿Qué tal?
See you later	Hasta luego
Sorry	Lo siento/ disculpeme
Excuse me	Con permiso/perdón
How are you?	¿Cómo está (usted)?
Not at all/ You're welcome	De nada
I (don't) understand	(No) Entiendo
Do you speak English?	¿Habla (usted) inglés?
I don't speak Spanish	(No) Hablo español
What (did you say)?	Mande?
My name is...	Me llamo...
What's your name?	¿Como se llama usted?
I am English	Soy inglés(a)
...American	...americano(a)
...Australian	...australiano(a)
...Canadian	...canadiense(a)
...Irish	...irlandés(a)
...New Zealander	...neozelandés(a)
...Scottish	...escosés(a)
...Welsh	...galés(a)

Hotels, transport and directions

I want...	Quiero...
I'd like...	Quisiera... por favor
Do you know...?	¿Sabe...?
I don't know	No sé
There is... (Is there...?)	(¿)Hay... (?)
Give me...	Dame...
...(one like that)	...(uno así)
Do you have...?	¿Tiene...?
...the time	...la hora
...a room	...un cuarto
...with two beds/	...con dos camas/
...double bed	...cama matrimonial
It's for one person	Es para una persona
...(two people)	...(dos personas)
...for one night	...para una noche

...(one week)	...(una semana)
It's fine, how much is it?	¿Está bien, cuánto es?
It's too expensive	Es demasiado caro
Don't you have anything cheaper?	¿No tiene algo más barato?
Can one...?	¿Se puede...?
...camp (near) here?	¿...acampar aquí (cerca)?
Is there a hotel nearby?	¿Hay un hotel aquí cerca?
How do I get to...?	¿Por dónde se va a...?
Left, right, straight on	Izquierda, derecha, derecho
Where is...?	¿Dónde está...?
...the bus station	...la camionera central
...the railway station	...la estación de ferrocarriles
...the nearest bank	...el banco más cercano
...the ATM	...el cajero automático
...the post office	...el correo (la oficina de correos)
...the toilet	...el baño/sanitario
Where does the bus to . . . leave from?	¿De dónde sale el bus para . . .?
I'd like a (return) ticket to...	Quisiera un boleto (de ida y vuelta) para . . .
What time does it leave (arrive in...)?	¿A qué hora sale (llega en...)?
What is there to eat?	¿Qué hay para comer?
What's that?	¿Qué es eso?
What's this called in Spanish?	¿Cómo se llama este en español?

Numbers and days

1	un/uno/una
2	dos
3	tres
4	cuatro
5	cinco
6	seis
7	siete
8	ocho
9	nueve
10	diez
11	once
12	doce
13	trece

14	catorce	700	setecientos
15	quince	1000	mil
16	dieciséis	2000	dos mil
17	diecisiete		
20	veinte	first	primero/a
21	veintiuno	second	segundo/a
30	treinta	third	tercero/a
40	cuarenta	fifth	quinto/a
50	cincuenta	tenth	decimo/a
60	sesenta		
70	setenta	Monday	lunes
80	ochenta	Tuesday	martes
90	noventa	Wednesday	miércoles
100	cien(to)	Thursday	jueves
101	ciento uno	Friday	viernes
200	doscientos	Saturday	sábado
500	quinientos	Sunday	domingo

Menu reader

On the table

Azúcar	Sugar
Cuchara	Spoon
Cuchillo	Knife
Cuenta	Bill
Mantequilla	Butter
Pan	Bread
Pimienta	Pepper
Queso	Cheese
Sal	Salt
Salsa	Sauce
Servilleta	Napkin
Tenedor	Fork

Cooking terms

Asado/a	Broiled
Al horno/horneado	Baked
A la tampiqueña	Meat in thin strips served with guacamole and enchiladas
A la veracruzana	Usually fish, cooked with tomatoes, onions and green olives
En mojo de ajo	Fried with slow-cooked garlic
Barbacoa/pibil	Wrapped in leaves and herbs and steamed/cooked in a pit
Con mole	In *mole* sauce, based on a rich spice paste – *mole poblano* (with bitter chocolate) is the most common
A la parilla	Grilled over charcoal
A la plancha	Grilled on a hot plate
Empanizado/a	Breaded
Frito	Fried
Poco hecho/ a punto/ bien cocido	Rare/medium/ well done

Breakfast

Chilaquiles	Tortilla strips with shredded chicken and tomato sauce
Huevos…	Eggs
…a la Mexicana	…scrambled with tomato, onion and chile
…con jamón	…with ham
…con tocino	…with bacon
…motuleños	…fried, served on a tortilla with beans, ham, cheese, tomato sauce, peas and fried sweet plantains
…rancheros	…fried, served on a tortilla and covered in hot chile sauce
…revueltos	…scrambled
…tibios	…lightly boiled
Pan dulce	Pastries

Soups (sopas) and starters

Botana	Any snack served with drinks; free at traditional bars
Caldo	Broth (with bits in)
Ceviche	Raw fish pieces, marinated in lime juice
Entremeses	Hors d'oeuvres
Sopa...	Soup
...de frijoles	Creamy black-bean soup
...de lima	Chicken soup with tortilla strips and lime
...de verduras	Vegetable soup

Tortilla and corn dishes (antojitos)

Chiles rellenos	Stuffed peppers
Enchiladas	Rolled-up tacos, covered in chile sauce and baked
Enchiladas suizas	As above, with green chile and cheese
Flautas	Small rolled tortillas filled with red meat or chicken and then fried
Molletes	Split roll covered in beans and melted cheese, often with ham and avocado
Panuchos	Like salbutes, but with black beans as well
Quesadillas	Toasted or fried tortillas topped with cheese
Queso fundido	Melted cheese, served with tortillas and salsa
Salbutes	Crisp-fried tortillas topped with shredded turkey, lettuce, avocado and pickled onions
Tacos	Soft corn tortillas with filling
Tacos arabes/ al pastor	Tacos filled with spicy pork, sometimes served with a slice of pineapple

Tacos dorados	Deep-fried meat tacos
Tamales	Corn-meal pudding, stuffed with meat and steamed or baked in banana leaves
Torta	Bread roll filled with meat, lettuce and avocado
Tostadas	Flat crisp tortillas piled with meat and salad
Totopos	Crisp-fried tortilla wedges, served with salsa

Fish and seafood (pescados y mariscos)

Calamares	Squid
Camarones	Prawns
Cangrejo	Crab
Caracol	Conch
Cazón	Shark
Coctel	Seafood served in a tall glass with a spicy tomato sauce and avocado
Corvina	Sea bass
Filete entero	Whole, filleted fish
Huachinango	Red snapper
Langosta	Rock lobster
Merluza	Hake
Ostión	Oyster
Pezespada	Swordfish
Pulpo	Octopus

Meat (carne) and poultry (aves)

Alambre	Kebab
Albóndigas	Meatballs
Arrachera	Skirt steak
Barbacoa	Barbecued meat
Bistec	Steak (not always beef)
Cabeza	Head
Cabrito	Kid
Carne (de res)	Beef
Carne adobado	Barbecued/spicily stewed meat
Carnitas	Pork cooked with garlic until crispy
Cerdo	Pork
Chivo	Goat
Chorizo	Spicy sausage
Chuleta	Chop (usually pork)

Codorniz	Quail
Conejo	Rabbit
Cordero	Lamb
Costilla	Rib
Filete	Tenderloin/fillet
Guisado	Stew
Hígado	Liver
Lengua	Tongue
Lomo	Loin (of pork)
Milanesa	Breaded escalope
Pata	Feet
Pato	Duck
Pavo	Turkey
Pechuga	Breast
Pierna	Leg
Pollo	Chicken
Salchicha	Sausage or hot dog
Salpicón	Shredded beef and sliced radishes seasoned with vinegar
Ternera	Veal
Tripa	Tripe
Venado	Venison

Vegetables (verduras)

Aguacate	Avocado
Arroz	Rice
Betabel	Beetroot (often as a juice)
Calabacita	Zucchini (courgette)
Calabaza	Squash
Cebolla	Onion
Champiñones	Mushrooms
Chícharos	Peas
Col	Cabbage
Elote	Corn on the cob
Espinacas	Spinach
Flor de calabaza	Squash blossoms
Frijoles	Beans
Hongos	Mushrooms
Huitlacoche	Corn fungus, "Mexican truffles"
Jitomate	Tomato
Lechuga	Lettuce
Lentejas	Lentils
Nopales	Cactus paddle, usually roasted or pickled
Papas	Potatoes
Rajas	Strips of mild green poblano pepper
Zanahoria	Carrot

Fruits (fruta) and juice (jugo)

Cherimoya	Custard apple (sweetsop)
Ciruela	Plum
Coco	Coconut
Durazno	Peach
Frambuesa	Raspberry
Fresa	Strawberry
Guanábana	Soursop, like a large custard apple
Guayaba	Guava
Higo	Fig
Limón	Lime
Mamey	Like a large zapote, with sweet pink flesh reminiscent of sweet potato
Melón	Melon
Naranja	Orange
Papaya	Papaya
Piña	Pineapple
Pitahaya	Dragonfruit, type of cactus fruit with a mild, tangy taste
Plátano	Banana/plantain
Sandía	Watermelon
Toronja	Grapefruit
Tuna	Prickly pear (cactus fruit)
Uva	Grape
Zapote	Sapodilla, fruit of the chicle tree

Drinks (bebidas)

Agua (mineral/con gas)	Water (Mineral/sparkling)
Café de la olla	Mexican-style coffee brewed in a clay pot
Cerveza	Beer
Chelada	Beer with lime juice, ice and salt
Michelada	Beer with spicy lime juice, ice and salt
Horchata	Creamy rice-milk drink, sometimes with coconut
Té	Tea
Vino	Wine

Sweets (dulces)

Cajeta	Caramel confection often served with...
...crepas	...pancakes

...churros	...cinnamon-covered fritters
Champola	Ice cream or sorbet in a tall glass filled with milk
Ensalada de frutas	Fruit salad
Flan	Crème caramel
Helado	Ice cream
Nieve	Sorbet
Paleta	Fruit popsicle
Raspada	Shaved ice with fruit syrup

Yucatecan specialities

Achiote	A spice paste made with orange annatto seeds and garlic
Adobo	A chile-based spice paste similar to achiote
Brazo de reina	Large tamal filled with pumpkin seeds and hard-boiled egg
Habañero	Small, extremely hot chile pepper, made into red and green salsas
Mondongo	Tripe stewed in achiote and bitter orange and green onions
Papadzules	Enchiladas filled with hard-cooked egg, topped with green pumpkin-seed sauce
Poc-chuc	Pork marinated in citrus juice, then grilled
Pollo en relleno negro	Chicken in a black, slightly burnt chile sauce
Puchero	Meaty stew with sweet potato seasoned with cinnamon and allspice
Tikin-xic	Fish with achiote and spices wrapped in banana leaves and grilled
Xnipek	Raw habañero salsa; literally "dog's nose", for the sweat it causes

Glossary

Ayuntamiento town hall/government.

Cantina bar, usually men-only.

Cenote underground water source in the Yucatán.

Chac Maya god of rain.

Chac-mool recumbent statue, possibly a sacrificial figure or messenger to the gods.

Comedor cheap restaurant, literally dining room.

Descompuesto out of order.

Ejido communal farmland.

Feria fair (market).

FONART government agency to promote crafts.

FONATUR government tourism agency.

Guayabera embroidered shirt, usually for men.

Hacienda estate or the big house on it.

Henequen hemp fibre, grown mainly in Yucatán, used to make rope.

Huipil Maya women's embroidered dress or blouse.

I.V.A. 15 percent value-added tax (VAT).

Kukulkán Maya name for Quetzalcoatl.

Malecón seafront promenade.

Maya tribe who inhabited Honduras, Guatemala and southeastern Mexico from earliest times, and still does.

Mestizo mixed race, of Indian and Spanish descent.

Mirador lookout point.

Muelle jetty or dock.

NAFTA the North American Free Trade Agreement including Mexico, the USA and Canada; see also TLC.

Palacio mansion, but not necessarily royal.

Palacio de Gobierno headquarters of state/federal authorities.

Palacio Municipal headquarters of local government.

Palapa palm thatch. Used to describe any thatched/palm-roofed hut.

Paseo a broad avenue, but also the ritual evening walk around the plaza.

Planta baja ground floor – abbreviated PB in lifts.

Quetzalcoatl the plumed serpent, most powerful, enigmatic and widespread of all ancient Mexican gods.

Sacbé ancient Maya road; plural *sacbeob*.

Stela freestanding carved monument.

TLC Tratado de Libre Comercio, the Spanish name for NAFTA.

Toltec tribe which controlled central Mexico between Teotihuacán and the Aztecs.

Trova Romantic Yucatecan song style popular in the early twentieth century, still played by *trovadores*.

Tula The Toltec capital.

Tzompantli Aztec skull rack or "wall of skulls".

Zócalo the main plaza of any town.

ROUGH GUIDES TRAVEL...

UK & Ireland
Britain
Devon & Cornwall
Dublin
Edinburgh
England
Ireland
Lake District
London
London
  DIRECTIONS
London Mini Guide
Scotland
Scottish Highlands
  & Islands
Wales

Europe
Algarve
Amsterdam
Amsterdam
  DIRECTIONS
Andalucía
Athens DIRECTIONS
Austria
Baltic States
Barcelona
Belgium &
  Luxembourg
Berlin
Brittany &
  Normandy
Bruges & Ghent
Brussels
Budapest
Bulgaria
Copenhagen
Corfu
Corsica
Costa Brava
Crete
Croatia
Cyprus
Czech & Slovak
  Republics
Dodecanese & East
  Aegean
Dordogne & The Lot
Europe
Florence
France

Germany
Greece
Greek Islands
Hungary
Ibiza & Formentera
Iceland
Ionian Islands
Italy
Languedoc &
  Roussillon
Lisbon
Lisbon DIRECTIONS
The Loire
Madeira
Madrid
Mallorca
Malta & Gozo
Menorca
Moscow
Netherlands
Norway
Paris
Paris DIRECTIONS
Paris Mini Guide
Poland
Portugal
Prague
Provence & the
  Côte d'Azur
Pyrenees
Romania
Rome
Sardinia
Scandinavia
Sicily
Slovenia
Spain
St Petersburg
Sweden
Switzerland
Tenerife & La
  Gomera
Tenerife
  DIRECTIONS
Turkey
Tuscany & Umbria
Venice & The
  Veneto
Venice DIRECTIONS
Vienna

Asia
Bali & Lombok
Bangkok
Beijing
Cambodia
China
Goa
Hong Kong &
  Macau
India
Indonesia
Japan
Laos
Malaysia, Singapore
  & Brunei
Nepal
Philippines
Singapore
South India
Southeast Asia
Sri Lanka
Thailand
Thailand's Beaches
  & Islands
Tokyo
Vietnam

Australasia
Australia
Melbourne
New Zealand
Sydney

North America
Alaska
Big Island of Hawaii
Boston
California
Canada
Chicago
Florida
Grand Canyon
Hawaii
Honolulu
Las Vegas
Los Angeles
Maui
Miami & the Florida
  Keys
Montréal

New England
New Orleans
New York City
New York City
  DIRECTIONS
New York City Mini
  Guide
Pacific Northwest
Rocky Mountains
San Francisco
San Francisco
  DIRECTIONS
Seattle
Southwest USA
Toronto
USA
Vancouver
Washington DC
Yosemite

**Caribbean
& Latin America**
Antigua & Barbuda
Antigua
  DIRECTIONS
Argentina
Bahamas
Barbados
Barbados
  DIRECTIONS
Belize
Bolivia
Brazil
Caribbean
Central America
Chile
Costa Rica
Cuba
Dominican Republic
Ecuador
Guatemala
Jamaica
Maya World
Mexico
Peru
St Lucia
South America
Trinidad & Tobago

Rough Guides are available from good bookstores worldwide. New titles are published every month. Check www.roughguides.com for the latest news.

...MUSIC & REFERENCE

Africa & Middle East
Cape Town
Egypt
The Gambia
Jordan
Kenya
Marrakesh DIRECTIONS
Morocco
South Africa, Lesotho & Swaziland
Syria
Tanzania
Tunisia
West Africa
Zanzibar
Zimbabwe

Travel Theme guides
First-Time Around the World
First-Time Asia
First-Time Europe
First-Time Latin America
Skiing & Snowboarding in North America
Travel Online
Travel Health
Walks in London & SE England
Women Travel

Restaurant guides
French Hotels & Restaurants
London
New York
San Francisco

Maps
Algarve
Amsterdam
Andalucia & Costa del Sol

Argentina
Athens
Australia
Baja California
Barcelona
Berlin
Boston
Brittany
Brussels
Chicago
Crete
Croatia
Cuba
Cyprus
Czech Republic
Dominican Republic
Dubai & UAE
Dublin
Egypt
Florence & Siena
Frankfurt
Greece
Guatemala & Belize
Iceland
Ireland
Kenya
Lisbon
London
Los Angeles
Madrid
Mexico
Miami & Key West
Morocco
New York City
New Zealand
Northern Spain
Paris
Peru
Portugal
Prague
Rome
San Francisco
Sicily
South Africa
South India
Sri Lanka
Tenerife
Thailand
Toronto

Trinidad & Tobago
Tuscany
Venice
Washington DC
Yucatán Peninsula

Dictionary Phrasebooks
Czech
Dutch
Egyptian Arabic
European Languages (Czech, French, German, Greek, Italian, Portuguese, Spanish)
French
German
Greek
Hindi & Urdu
Hungarian
Indonesian
Italian
Japanese
Mandarin Chinese
Mexican Spanish
Polish
Portuguese
Russian
Spanish
Swahili
Thai
Turkish
Vietnamese

Music Guides
The Beatles
Bob Dylan
Cult Pop
Classical Music
Country Music
Elvis
Hip Hop
House
Irish Music
Jazz
Music USA
Opera

Reggae
Rock
Techno
World Music (2 vols)

History Guides
China
Egypt
England
France
India
Islam
Italy
Spain
USA

Reference Guides
Books for Teenagers
Children's Books, 0–5
Children's Books, 5–11
Cult Fiction
Cult Football
Cult Movies
Cult TV
Ethical Shopping
Formula 1
The iPod, iTunes & Music Online
The Internet
Internet Radio
James Bond
Kids' Movies
Lord of the Rings
Muhammed Ali
Man Utd
Personal Computers
Pregnancy & Birth
Shakespeare
Superheroes
Unexplained Phenomena
The Universe
Videogaming
Weather
Website Directory

so! More than 120 Rough Guide music CDs are available from all good book and record stores. Listen in at www.worldmusic.net

small print & Index

A Rough Guide to Rough Guides

Cancun DIRECTIONS is published by Rough Guides. The first *Rough Guide to Greece*, published in 1982, was a student scheme that became a publishing phenomenon. The immediate success of the book – with numerous reprints and a Thomas Cook prize short-listing – spawned a series that rapidly covered dozens of destinations. Rough Guides had a ready market among low-budget backpackers, but soon also acquired a much broader and older readership that relished Rough Guides' wit and inquisitiveness as much as their enthusiastic, critical approach. Everyone wants value for money, but not at any price. Rough Guides soon began supplementing the "rougher" information about hostels and low-budget listings with the kind of detail on restaurants and quality hotels that independent-minded visitors on any budget might expect, whether on business in New York or trekking in Thailand. These days the guides offer recommendations from shoestring to luxury and cover a large number of destinations around the globe, including almost every country in the Americas and Europe, more than half of Africa and most of Asia and Australasia. Rough Guides now publish:

- Travel guides to more than 200 worldwide destinations
- Dictionary phrasebooks to 22 major languages
- Maps printed on rip-proof and waterproof Polyart™ paper
- Music guides running the gamut from Opera to Elvis
- Reference books on topics as diverse as the Weather and Shakespeare
- World Music CDs in association with World Music Network

Publishing information

This 1st edition published May 2005 by
Rough Guides Ltd, 80 Strand, London WC2R 0RL.
345 Hudson St, 4th Floor, New York, NY 10014,
USA.

Distributed by the Penguin Group
Penguin Books Ltd, 80 Strand, London WC2R 0RL
Penguin Group (USA), 375 Hudson St, NY 10014,
USA
Penguin Group (Australia), 250 Camberwell Rd,
Camberwell, Victoria 3124, Australia
Penguin Group (Canada), 10 Alcorn Ave, Toronto,
ON M4V 1E4, Canada
Penguin Group (New Zealand), Cnr Rosedale and
Airborne Roads, Albany, Auckland, New Zealand
Typeset in Bembo and Helvetica to an original
design by Henry Iles.
Printed and bound in China by Leo

© Zora O'Neill, May 2005

192pp includes index

A catalogue record for this book is available from
the British Library

ISBN 1-84353-400-2

1   3   5   7   9   8   6   4   2

Help us update

We've gone to a lot of effort to ensure that the first edition of **Cancun DIRECTIONS** is accurate and up-to-date. However, things change – places get "discovered", opening hours are notoriously fickle, restaurants and rooms raise prices or lower standards. If you feel we've got it wrong or left something out, we'd like to know, and if you can remember the address, the price, the phone number, so much the better.

We'll credit all contributions, and send a copy of the next edition (or any other DIRECTIONS guide or Rough Guide if you prefer) for the best letters. Everyone who writes to us and isn't already a subscriber will receive a copy of our full-colour thrice-yearly newsletter. Please mark letters: "**Cancun DIRECTIONS Update**" and send to: Rough Guides, 80 Strand, London WC2R 0RL, or Rough Guides, 4th Floor, 345 Hudson St, New York, NY 10014. Or send an email to **mail@roughguides.com**

Have your questions answered and tell others about your trip at **www.roughguides.atinfopop.com**

Rough Guide credits

Text editor: Steven Horak
Layout: Andy Hilliard, Dan May
Photography: Alex Robinson
Cartography: Animesh Pathak, Katie Lloyd-Jones, Maxine Repath

Picture editor: Joe Mee, Harriet Mills
Proofreader: Susannah Wight
Production: Julia Bovis
Design: Henry Iles
Cover design: Louise Boulton, Chloe Roberts, Dan May

The author

Zora O'Neill got her start advising travelers in a café in Amsterdam, where she was charged with dispensing tourist information the day after she arrived. She now has significantly more expertise and lives in New York City, travelling as often as possible, in an attempt to taste every food in the world. In addition to covering the Yucatán peninsula for Rough Guides, she writes about New York, Amsterdam, the Middle East and New Mexico, where she's originally from.

Acknowledgements

The author would like to thank: most certainly Steven Horak for painstaking editing and Alex Robinson for excellent photos and additional travel tips, as well as Claudia Barrera and Lennard Struyk, Ry Koteen, Stefania Cappelletti, Pia and Thed in Playa, Pedro and Eyal on Cozumel, Eliane Godement, Rob and Joanne Birce, Catriona Brown, Sandra Dayton, Andria Mitsakos, Stephanie Abrams, Janelle at Turquoise Reef, Curtis and Ashley Blogin, Jules Siegel, Claudia Pacheco, Lee Christie and *mi choffer* Pedro.

Photo credits

All images © Rough Guides except the following:

Title page: Hammocks on the beach, Cozumel © Charles Register/ALAMY
p.5 Tulum © ML Sinibaldi/CORBIS
p.6 Temazcal evening, Maroma Hotel © Orient-Express Hotels/Maroma Hotel
p.7 Divers in Marine Park, Cozumel © Carlos Villoch/ALAMY
p.8 View of El Castillo pyramid, Chichén Itzá © Mark Thomas
p.10 El Castillo © www.yupuri.com/Alex Robinson
p.10 Cancún coastline © CORBIS
p.11 Giant anemone and sea rod, near San Miguel de Cozumel © CORBIS
p.11 Cenote X-Keken, Dzitnup © Macduff Everton/CORBIS
p.11 Tulum view © Mark Thomas
p.14 Snorkelling near caves © Cancún Conventions and Visitors Bureau
p.14 Prow of Sunken C-53 Minesweeper © CORBIS
p.15 Queen angelfish © Dive Puerto Morelos
p. 15 Southern stingray and fish on the sea floor, near San Miguel de Cozumel © CORBIS
p.31 Maroma bedroom © Orient-Express Hotels/Maroma Hotel
p.31 Deseo © DK Images
p.32 Ek-Balam © www.yupuri.com/Alex Robinson
p.32 Detail of Mayan Sculpture at Tulum Ruins © Richard A. Cooke/CORBIS
p.33 Stone carving detail, sacrificial platform, Chichén Itzá © www.yupuri.com/Alex Robinson

p.34 Female green sea turtle returns to the Pacific Ocean © George H. H. Huey/CORBIS
p.35 Brown pelican © Tim Thompson/CORBIS
p.35 Spider monkey © Kevin Schafer/CORBIS
p.35 Fisherman over Boca Paila lagoon, Reserva de la Biósfera Sian Ka'an © Macduff Everton/CORBIS
p.36 Sailing near Cancún Isla Mujeres © Cancún Conventions and Visitors Bureau
p.37 Mayan village tour, Maya Echo eco-tour © Maya Echo
p. 37 Jungle buggy tour © Veronica Sanchez Withington/www.cozumelhomes.com
p. 37 Jungle tours © Goyo Morgan/Goyo's Jungle Tours
p.37 Aerial view of the coast of Cancún © Charles Lenars/CORBIS
p.38 Fishing for bonefish in a shallow lagoon © Boca Paila, Sian Ka'an Biosphere Reserve. © Macduff Everton/CORBIS
p.39 Snorkelling, Cancún © Cancún Conventions and Visitors Bureau
p.39 Kayaking in a mangrove swamp © Peter Guttman/CORBIS
p.39 Young woman surfing © CORBIS
p. 39 Kiteboarding, Cancún © Mexico Tourism Board
p.41 Plaza de Toros © Cancún Conventions and Visitors Bureau
p.41 Ballet Folklorico Nacional de Mexico © Lindsay Hebberd/CORBIS

Index

Maps are marked in colour

a

accommodation (by area)
Cancún's zona hotelera 57
Cozumel 122
Downtown Cancún 71
inland 153
Isla Mujeres 85
Playa del Carmen 104
Puerto Morelos 94
Tulum 136
accommodation
Acamaya Reef 94
Aguilar 122
Alhambra 104
Alux 71
Amar Inn 94
Ambiance Villas at Kin-Ha 57
Las Anclas 31, 122
Antillano 71
Aquamarina Beach Hotel 57
Aristos 57
Los Arrecifes 136
Avalon Baccará 57
Azulik 27, 136
Bahía Xcalacoco 94
Belmar 85
Boca Paila Camps 42, 136, 163
Cabañas Copal 136
Cabañas El Mirador 138
Cabañas La Ruina 104
Cabañas Zazil-Kin 138
La Candelaria 153
Cancún Inn El Patio 71
Cancún Rosa 71
Caribe Blu 122
Casa de Las Flores 104
Casa Maya Zazil-Há 85
Casa Mexicana 123
Casa Tucan 104
Ceiba del Mar 94
Chac Mool Hostel 71
Chichen 72
Coco's Cabañas 29, 95
Colonial 72
Cristalmar 85
El Crucero 138
Deseo 31, 105
Dolores Alba 153
Dreams Cancun 57
Flamingo 123
Francis Arlene 85
Genesis Ek Balam 154, 163
Grand Royal Lagoon 58
Hacienda Cancún 72
Hotelito Sac-bé 154
Imperial Laguna 58
Kin Mayab 72
Kinbé 31, 105

Le Meridien 30, 58
L'Hotelito 138
Lunata 105
Mar y Sol 86
María Guadalupe 154
Maroma 31, 95
Marruang 123
Maya Echo B&B 95
El Mesón del Marqués 154
Mexico Hostel 72
Na Balam 86
Nueva Vida de Ramiro 29, 138
Ojo de Agua 96
Palapas Amaranto 123
Palma Dorada 123
Las Palmas 72
Papaya Playa 139
El Paraíso 139
Pepita 123
Playa Azul 123
Playa la Media Luna 86
Posada Amor 96
La Posada del Capitán Lafitte 45, 96
La Posada del Sol 139
Posada El Moro 96
Posada Freud 105
Posada Isla Mujeres 86
Posada Mariposa 105
El Presidente Inter-Continental (Cancún) 58, 124
El Pueblito 59
Punta Allen 73
La Rana Cansada 106
Rancho Tranquilo 140
Las Ranitas 140
El Rey del Caribe 73
Ritz-Carlton Cancún 59
Roca Mar 86
Sak Ol 29, 96
Secreto 85
Shangri-La Caribe 106
Sheraton Cancún Resort & Towers 59
Sol Cabañas del Caribe 124
Suites Girasol 59
Suites Los Arcos 86
Suites Sina 59
Sunscape Tulum 45, 140
Tamarindo 29, 124
Tribal Village 139
Ventanas al Mar 43, 125
Villa Las Brisas 28, 86
Villas Arqueológicas 154
Villas Manglar 59
Villas Tacul 60
Vista del Mar 125
Westin Resort & Spa Cancún 60
Zací 154
Zamas 140
La Ziranda 106

airlines 170
airports 53, 70, 113, 159
airplane tours 37, 161
all-inclusive resorts 163
Avenida 5 (La Quinta) 11, 99
Avenida Yaxchilán 70
Aviario Xaman-Ha 103

b

Ballet Folklórico Nacional de México 41, 66
bars and lounges (by area)
Cancún's zona hotelera 64
Cozumel 130
Downtown Cancún 77
inland 155
Isla Mujeres 89
Playa del Carmen 111
Puerto Morelos 98
Tulum 143
bars and lounges
Ambar 130
Arrecife 89
Bally-Hoo 89
Bar Ranita 111
Buho's 89
El Camarote 16, 76
Capitán Tutix 111
La Casa 940 77
Charlie's 143
El Chat 77
Don Pepe Olé 98
Dragon Bar 111
Hard Rock Café 64
Havana Club 130
Hemingway 89
Kartabar 111
Kelley's 130
Le Hooka 77
Lobby Bar at the Ritz-Carlton 64
La Madonna 26, 64
Oasis Azul 143
Om 89
Pat O'Brien's 64
Papaya Playa 17, 139
El Paraíso Beach Club 143
La Peña 89
Señor Frog's 64
El Tigre 111
Tony Rome's Embassy 130
Trágara 17, 64
Ula-Gula 16, 111
La Vita è Bella 143
Yepez II 155
bargaining 170
baseball 46, 71, 168
beaches and beach clubs

INDEX

(by area)
Cancún 10, 54
Cozumel 119
Isla Mujeres 80, 82
Playa del Carmen 99
Puerto Morelos 93, 94
Tulum 134
beaches and beach clubs
Caleta Tankah 134
Chen Río 12, 121
Dzul-Ha 119
Eastern coast (Cozumel) 12, 121
Mamita's 12, 101
Mar Caribe 134
Nachi-Cocom 13, 120
Paradise Beach 120
El Paraíso 13,134
Playa Acamaya 93
Playa Azul 119
Playa Caribe 99
Playa Delfines 13, 55
Playa Lancheros 23, 82
Playa Langosta 53
Playa Maya 134
Playa Mirador 56
Playa Norte 13, 80
Playa Palancar 120
Playa Tortugas 53
Playa Xcalacoco 94
Punta Brava 93
Punta Zubul 101
bicycles 161
bowling 171
buses 70, 78, 91, 99, 113, 131, 144, 160,

c

cafés (by area)
Cancún's zona hotelera 61
Cozumel 126
Downtown Cancún 74
inland 154
Isla Mujeres 87
Playa del Carmen 108
Puerto Morelos 97
Tulum 141
cafés
El Café 74
Café Cito 87
Café de Carmelita 154
Café Sasta 108
Los Cántaros 141
Carmencita 108
La Casa del Buen Pan 141
Cazuela M&J 87
Chaya's Natural Restaurant 154
Chilangos 126
Cocktelería Picus 22, 87
Coco's 126
Coffeelia 126
La Cueva del Chango 42, 108
Del Museo 126

El D'Pa 74
Dub 74
La Flor de Michoacan 141
La Floresta 22, 108
Garden of Eatin' 126
La Guadalupana II 97
Hot 109
Jeanie's Waffles 126
Mama's 97
La Nave 141
Nieve de Dioses 75
El Oasis 109
El Pabilo 75
Pan de Carmen 109
Panadería Cozumeleña 126
El Picudo Azul 97
Rock'n Java 127
Serious Munchies 127
Super-Hit Tortas 127
El Tío 97
Tuti Fruti 141
Ty-Coz 61, 75
Zermatt 127
Canal Sigfrido 53
Cancún downtown 67
Cancún, downtown 68
Cancún's zona hotelera 51
Cancún's zona hotelera 52
car rental 160
Carnaval 47, 168
Casa del Arte Popular Mexicano, La 51
cave diving 14, 39, 135
Cedral, El 118
cenotes 6, 11
Carwash (Aktun-Ha) 134
Casa Cenote 135
Dzitnup 151
Gran Cenote 134
Hidden Worlds 135
Ruta de los Cenotes 91
Samula 151
Chankanaab 44, 119
Chichén Itzá 8, 10, 33, 147
Chichén Itzá 148
cinemas 171
clubs (by area)
Cancún's zona hotelera 65
Cozumel 130
Downtown Cancún 77
Isla Mujeres 89
Playa del Carmen 111
clubs
Alux 27, 111
Azúcar 65
Batacha 65
La Boom 65
Bulldog Café 65
City, The 18, 65
Coco Bongo 19, 65
Glazz 19, 65
G-Spot 66
Karamba 77
Mambo Café 19, 77, 112
Nitrox Club VIP 89
Over 30 Club 66
Roots 17, 77

Royal Bandstand, The 66
La Santanera 19, 112
La Tramoya 77
Viva México 130
Cobá 33, 152
colectivos 144, 160
consulates 171
coral reefs 5, 15, 51, 53, 118, 165, 190
Cozumel, Isla 113
Cozumel, Isla 114
Crucero, El (Downtown Cancún) 70
Cuevas de los Tiburones Dormidos 14, 83

d

Día de los Muertos (Day of the Dead) 47, 169
Día de la Independencia (Independence Day) 46, 168
disabled travellers 171
dive shops 166
diving 14, 165

e

ecoresorts 163
Ek-Balam 32, 151
electricity 171
emergencies 171
equinoxes 47, 168

f

ferries 78, 94, 113, 161
festivals and events 46, 168
fishing 38, 167
food, Yucatecan 164, 180

g

Garrafón 82
gay and lesbian travellers 171
golf 167
Gran Meliá Cancún 55
Grutas de Balankanché 150

h

Hacienda Mundaca 82
hammocks 21, 74, 107, 170

hotels *see accommodation*
huipiles 169

i

Iglesia de San Miguel 40, 115
Internet cafés 171
Isla Contoy 35, 84
Isla Mujeres 78
Isla Mujeres 79
Isla Mujeres, Punta Norte 81
Isla Mujeres (town) 78

j

Jardín Botánico Dr Alfredo
  Barrera Marín 92
jet skiing 37, 167
jungle tours 167

k

kayaking 39, 135
kiteboarding 39, 93, 166

l

luggage storage 171

m

mail and post offices 171
mangroves 34, 53, 93, 167
maps and media 159
Maya, the 56, 118–119,
  131–134, 144, 146–153
menu items 177
Mesoamerican Barrier Reef
  90, 165
money 162
monkey reserve 153
Museo de la Isla de Cozumel
  40, 115
Museo INAH 54

p

parasailing 167
Parque Central (Playa del
  Carmen) 101
Parque de las Palapas 23, 67
Parque Marino Nacional
  Arrecifes de Cozumel 118
Parque Nacional Arrecifes de
  Puerto Morelos 90
Parque Nizuc 57
Parque Punta Sur 34, 121
pharmacies 171
Playacar 102
Playa Acamaya 93
Playa Azul 119
Playa Caribe 99
Playa Delfines 13, 55
Playa Lancheros 23, 82
Playa Langosta 53
Playa Maya 134
Playa Mirador 56
Playa Norte 13, 80
Playa Palancar 120
Playa Tortugas 53
Playa Xcalacoco 94
Playa del Carmen 99
Playa del Carmen 100
Playa del Carmen, greater
  102
Plaza de Toros 41, 70
public holidays 169
Puerto Morelos 90
Puerto Morelos 92
Puerto Morelos coast 90
Punta Cancún 53
Punta Nizúc 53

r

Reserva de la Biósfera Sian
  Ka'an 35, 135
restaurants (by area)
  Cancún's zona hotelera 62
  Cozumel 127
  Downtown Cancún 75
  inland 155
  Isla Mujeres 87
  Playa del Carmen 109
  Puerto Morelos 97
  Tulum 141
restaurants
  restaurants
  100% Natural 61, 75, 109
  Los Almendros 75, 109
  Babe's 109
  El Bazar 155
  Buenos Aires 110
  Caffé del Puerto 97
  Captain Hook 66
  La Casa de las Margaritas
    25, 62
  Casa Denis 127
  Casa Rolandi 27, 62, 87
  Cetli 141
  Checándole 62, 76
  La Choza 127
  Conchita del Caribe 128
  La Destilería 62
  Dolcemente Pompei 62
Don Huacho del 1/2 Dia 141
El Tacoqueto 142
El Turix 129
Especias 128
El Faisán y El Venado 110
El Galeón del Caribe 63
La Habichuela 24, 76
Hanaichi 63
Hechizo 142
Hola Asia 98
Hola Primo 142
Hostería El Marqués 155
Los Huaraches de Alcatraces
  76
Jax Bar & Grill 87
JC Capitán 63
John Gray's Kitchen 25, 98
John Gray's Place 110
Labná 76
Le Bistro Français 87
La Lobstería 128
La Lomita 88
Lonchería Alexía y Geovanny
  88
María de la Luz 155
Media Luna 110
La Morena 128
El Olivo 110
Osteria La Rucola 110
Pancho's Backyard 25, 128
Pericos 76
La Petita 98
La Pirámide 155
El Pirata 98
Pollos Asados Doña Rosa 142
Posada Margherita 25, 142
Prima 129
Qué Fresco 142
Restaurante San Bernardino
  de Siena 155
El Rincón Yucateco 63, 76
Río Nizúc 63
Rolandi's 88
Rosa Mexicano 76
Sabores 23, 129
Salus y Chemo's 76
El Sombrero d'Gomar 88
Spaghettino 98
Taquería Díaz 142
La Tarraya 110
Velazquez 88
La Veranda 129
Yaxche 24, 111
Zazil Ha 88
resorts 163
Rey, El 35, 56

s

sailing 36, 167
San Gervasio 33, 118
San Miguel 113
San Miguel, downtown 116
scuba diving *see diving*
shopping 20, 169

192

shops (by area)
Cancún's zona hotelera 60
Cozumel 125
Downtown Cancún 73
Isla Mujeres 86
Playa del Carmen 106
Puerto Morelos 96
Tulum 140
shops
El Aguacate 21, 74
Alma Libre 21, 96
Ambar Mexicano 106
Artesanías Glenssy 86
La Calaca 20, 106
Casita de la Musica 107
Los Cinco Soles 20, 125
Coral Negro 60
Fama 73
Hunab-Ku Artesanía 97
Idé 107
Indigo 125
La Isla Shopping Village 60
Joyería Posada del Sol 140
Juan's Hammocks 107
Ki-Huic 73
Lu'um K'aa Nab Artesanía 97
Maya Art 107
Mercado 23 21, 73
Mercado 28 73
Mercado Municipal (Cozumel) 115
Mixik Artesanías 140
Paseo del Carmen 21, 107
Plaza Bonita 74
Plaza Caracol 61

Plaza Kukulcán 61
Pygmees 107
Qué Pequeño es el Mundo 107
Rachat & Romero 125
La Rana Sabia 75
U'nahi Pax 125
Sian Ka'an Biosphere Reserve 35, 135
snorkelling 14, 165
Spanish 175
spas 171
sports 165

t

taxis 161
Teatro de Cancún 66
telephones 172
Templo de Ixchel 83
time 172
tipping 172
tour operators 161
tourist offices 78, 91, 99, 113, 31, 144
travel agents 172
Tulum 131
Tulum, around 132
Tulum ruins 11, 32, 131
Tulum town 137

V

Valladolid 144
Valladolid 146
visas and passports 172

W

weather 6
water sports 38, 166
websites 159
windsurfing 167

X

Xcaret 45, 103
Xel-Há Ecopark 135
Xel-Há ruins 135

y

Yamil Lu'um 55
yoga 167

INDEX